NAZISM 1918-1945

NAZISM 1918-1945

by

M. J. THORNTON

Senior History Teacher
Bramcote Hills Grammar School, Nottinghamshire

PERGAMON PRESS

OXFORD · LONDON · EDINBURGH · NEW YORK
TORONTO · PARIS · FRANKFURT

Pergamon Press Ltd., Headington Hill Hall, Oxford
4 & 5 Fitzroy Square, London, W.1

Pergamon Press (Scotland) Ltd., 2 & 3 Teviot Place, Edinburgh 1

Pergamon Press Inc., 44-01 21st Street, Long Island City, New York 11101

Pergamon of Canada Ltd., 6 Adelaide Street East, Toronto, Ontario

Pergamon Press S.A.R.L., 24 rue des Ecoles, Paris 5e

Pergamon Press GmbH, Kaiserstrasse 75, Frankfurt-am-Main

Printed in Great Britain by Billing and Sons Limited, Guildford and London

Contents

Preface

THE literature of Nazism is considerable, and to add to it requires some word of explanation. It is the existence of so many large books on the subject which, I believe, justifies this small one.

The modern student, whether in the Sixth Form or at Training College or the University, is constantly exhorted to read widely inside and outside his chosen field. The demands made on him in this way are at times quite unrealistic, since the appropriate type of book is often non-existent.

Most sixth-formers, reading history, need to absorb a firm outline of their period before the acknowledged works of scholarship are of any use to them. The same is often true of students at even higher levels. The case of the science student, who is expected to bridge the two cultures, is even more unenviable. The expanding scope of his own field leaves him with precious little time to devote to any other. Those who doubt the truth of this should take an honest look at our maintained grammar schools and universities.

It is my hope, therefore, that this book will not only provide a comprehensible introduction to the history of Nazism, but will stimulate and enable those who use it to investigate the subject more deeply. To this end I have included a short list of further reading.

This book is based on the research of others to whom I freely acknowledge my debt, and the pleasure I have derived from their work.

Finally, I express my gratitude to my wife, who produced the typescript, and corrected my English and punctuation, under conditions far from ideal. Any mistakes which remain are my own.

M.J.T.

CHAPTER ONE

A View of Life

THIRTY THOUSAND Nazis raised their arms in salute to Adolf Hitler, their leader, now Chancellor and Reichsfuehrer of Germany, as he marched down the aisle of the Luitpold Hall in Nuremberg on the morning of 5th September 1933. The Party Congress was assembled to hear his proclamation, read to them by Adolf Wagner, *Gauleiter** of Bavaria. The German way of life, the Fuehrer had written, was determined for the next thousand years. In May 1945 the Third Reich passed into oblivion. Its destruction had cost nearly fifty million lives and material loss and human suffering beyond calculation.

To those who have reached maturity since 1945 it is almost as though Nazism had never existed. Only outbreaks of swastika daubing, the posturings of a few extremists in Trafalgar Square, or, more seriously, Reuter reports of S.S. reunions in Munich and the trial of Adolf Eichmann in Jerusalem, occur to perpetuate its memory. Yet a knowledge of it is one of history's clearest warnings of what can happen to the world when men forget their common humanity.

Whether or not Nazism had, in the strict sense of the words, a philosophy or ideology, has been disputed during its lifetime and since its destruction; and even if it had such a body of doctrine, it is debatable whether this had any relevance to the course of action followed after 1933.

Certainly the movement was anti-intellectual, and not based on a closely reasoned body of dogma as Communism to some

---

* See p. 33.

I

extent is. Nor did the opinions of the Nazi leaders provide them
with a detailed blueprint for the policies they pursued when in
power. On the other hand, they did hold opinions which provided
a general basis and justification for their actions, and, in contrast
to Fascism, these opinions preceded political action. Nor can they
be brushed aside only as useful instruments of propaganda. These
they certainly proved to be, but there is no reason to suppose that
the authors of *Mein Kampf*, or the *Myth of the Twentieth Century*, did not sincerely hold the views they expressed. Indeed
Hitler emphasized the importance of what he called *Weltanschauung*. Almost untranslatable, this word means 'a view of
life'. It is the general outlook, or everyday 'philosophy', not
closely based on rational thought, which most of us have. The
consistency with which Hitler clung to his *weltanschauung* is
in marked contrast to the opportunism of his career as a politician.

Adolf Hitler's autobiographical *Mein Kampf*, written during his
confinement in the Landsberg Fortress Prison after his failure to
seize power in 1923, and Alfred Rosenberg's pretentious *Myth of
the Twentieth Century* are the two most significant works ex-
pressing what Nazism was in the minds of its leaders. Neither is a
scholarly work by any exacting criteria. The authors selected
quite at random such items from other works as would support
their own ingrained prejudices. Hitler may have been a voracious
reader, but it is not clear what he read, and his standards of
scholarship are made apparent in his own words : '. . . one who
has cultivated the art of reading will instantly discern . . . what
ought to be remembered because it meets one's personal needs or
is of value as general knowledge'. Thus it is, for example, that
although the ideas of Nietzsche have been regarded as one of the
roots of Nazism, and the Nazis themselves were not averse to
acknowledging such antecedents, only select anthologies of his
work circulated in Nazi Germany. Hitler was not loth to see
himself in the role of the heroic leader of the masses, but
Nietzsche's contempt for nationalism and his moderate attitude
towards the Jews, were at variance with Nazi requirements and

accordingly suppressed. Rosenberg elaborated his version of history with disregard for the available anthropological, biological and historical evidence which refutes his opinions. On the contrary, he relied heavily on the nineteenth-century works of the Comte de Gobineau and H. S. Chamberlain, neither of whom could claim scientific or historical training.

In this tendentious manner the ideas behind Nazism took shape. Its name is misleading since it was concerned neither with nationalism nor with socialism as these are commonly understood. A number of unfulfilled promises in the original Party Programme, drawn up in 1920, was its socialism. Only as a means to attract mass support were they of significance. Only in the sense that their ambitions presupposed political control over the nation's economy were the Nazis socialists. Egalitarianism, and the removal of economic and social injustice were humanitarian aims beneath their contempt.

Nor was nationalism conceived of in terms of existing political frontiers, or even of previously existing ones. The nation was not, in Nazi theory, a society of mixed origins bound together by a way of life. Modern America provides an example of what we might regard as a nation. Although their forefathers came from every part of the globe, Americans exhibit today a strong sense of solidarity as a nation. Such a society could never have been other than a mongrel agglomeration in the eyes of Rosenberg. The Nazis exalted the *Volk*, or folk, a people of unmixed racial origins who were mystically bound together in a primitive community of blood and soil which recognized no artificial boundaries: an emotionally charged concept at variance with the political realities of post 1918 Europe.

The framework of the Nazi *weltanschauung*, as expressed by Hitler, was one of conflict, *Mein Kampf* means 'my struggle', and struggle is a word that recurred time and again in the writings and speeches of the Nazi leader:

'The whole work of Nature is a mighty struggle between strength and weakness . . . States which offend against this elementary law fall into decay.'

This struggle Hitler regarded as the basis of everything men had accomplished, and without it '. . . a man would . . . achieve nothing'. Hence humanitarianism was weakness in disguise, and 'in perpetual peace man's greatness must decline'. He held invalid any ideas of natural right, whether applied to men or nations, and this was thought to be in accord with divine justice:

'. . . there can be no miracle . . . which gives to a man anything he himself has not earned. Heaven at all times has helped only the man who has exerted himself.'

The outstanding feature of the Nazi *weltanschauung* was its insistence on race, and it was as a pattern of inter-racial struggle that Rosenberg re-interpreted history. Rosenberg was no more than a peripheral figure when the movement was in the heyday of its power, but he had joined the National-Socialist Party soon after its foundation and at one time enjoyed the status of being its semi-official philosopher; in 1921 he became the editor of the movement's leading newspaper, the *Voelkischer Beobachter*.

The struggle that Rosenberg perceived running through history had taken place between the Nordic or Aryan master race, and lesser breeds of mankind. The word 'race', used without precise biological meaning, and a spurious claim to descend from an alleged Aryan master race, may have originated with the Comte de Gobineau. The latter, in his *The Inequality of the Human Race*, had used the idea, in the middle of the nineteenth century, to support aristocracy against democracy. At the turn of the century, Houston Stewart Chamberlain, an Englishman who became Richard Wagner's son-in-law and adopted Germany as his country, popularized the Aryan myth there in a pseudo-scientific book *The Foundations of the Nineteenth Century*. The vital contribution made by Chamberlain was to elevate the existing cult of Germanism into a claim to national superiority. Gobineau had asserted the superiority of a social class; Chamberlain the superiority of a people over the rest of mankind.

Rosenberg held that the Aryan race had originated in Northern Europe, dispersing from there into Egypt, Persia, India, Greece and Rome. The only race with the power to create culture, it had fashioned the ancient civilizations which flourished in those areas. Their collapse, he argued, had been due to degeneracy that set in when the Aryans interbred with inferior races. In Europe the collapse of the Roman Empire had left behind racial confusion, and the struggle between this and the Teutonic Aryans had produced all that was good in modern art, philosophy, science, and political institutions. Christianity was corrupt — Rosenberg was virulently anti-Catholic — but Christ was an Aryan, and what was worth preserving in Christianity reflected, Rosenberg thought, Aryan ideals.

The philosophy on which this view of history was based rendered it unassailable from the author's point of view. The idea of an absolute truth he rejected completely, claiming that his essential message would not be discredited '. . . if the entire historical proof were to be refuted at every point'. He believed that all mental and moral faculties were racial, so that the Aryan intuitively knows what the essential truth is for him. 'We think with our blood', was the answer to any critic seeking cogent argument based consistently on factual evidence.

Rosenberg identified his Aryan race as fair, blue-eyed, tall and long-headed. Its personal characteristics included among others, honour, courage, love of freedom, and a spirit of scientific research. The mental and physical features were thought not always to correspond, and the exact boundaries of the race were left vague. After the Nazis came to power the theory was developed as 'scientific' anthropology, but with disregard for such anthropological information as skin-colour and hair.

The anti-race, and the cause of so much that Rosenberg thought degenerate, were the Jews. The inhuman persecution of the Jews that the Nazis carried out was firmly based on their view of life. That they were able to preach anti-semitism so openly before they came to power indicates how deep rooted it was as a social prejudice in central Europe.

What is pathetic about Rosenberg is his belief in his racial theory. In contrast, Hitler appreciated that it had no scientific basis, but perceived its value as a myth to be used. As he admitted to Hermann Rauschning:

'The conception of the nation is meaningless. We have to get rid of this false conception, and set in its place the conception of race. The new order cannot be conceived in terms of the natural boundaries of the peoples with an historic past but in terms of race that transcend these boundaries. . . . I know perfectly well that in the scientific sense there is no such thing as race, but you, as a farmer, cannot get your breeding successfully achieved without the conception of race. And I as a politician need a conception which enables the order which has hitherto existed on historic bases to be abolished, and an entirely new and anti-historic order enforced and given an intellectual basis. . . . With the conception of race National-Socialism will carry its revolution abroad and re-cast the world.'

In this conception of race the Aryans were only a part of any, even the German nation, and their role was to form an élite whose responsibility was to stamp its *weltanschauung* on the nation, giving the whole an Aryan character. This mythical concept justified the right of the Nazis to rule the Germans, and of the Germans to rule the Slavs. It also implied what, to Hitler, was an iron law of nature, that there is no equality between races or individual men.

From accepting the view of history as a racial struggle it is a natural step to exalt the *Volk*, and this entity formed the core of Hitler's beliefs. The well-being of the *Volk* he regarded as of overriding importance. The state was an artificial organism existing to preserve the *Volk*, rather than the other way round. Thus were justified early Nazi attacks on the Weimar government, which was accused of not protecting the *Volk* when 'the task of government is the maintenance of the people, the protection of the race . . . all its other tasks are conditioned by this primary duty'. The central position of the *Volk* also dictated the main function of the Party as an expression of its will, and necessitated the subordination of individual will and freedom to its service. Truth and justice were thought of as mere instruments with which the needs of the people could be served, and Hitler affirmed that: 'Justice is a means of ruling. Conscience is a Jewish invention. It is a blemish. . . .'

Hitler argued that the true interests of the *Volk* could never be preserved through democratic forms of government. Secret ballot, majority decisions and allied processes weakened the individual's responsibility to the *Volk*, and destroyed the heroic qualities which were characteristic of the Aryan race. Free expression and debate only sow seeds of doubt in the minds of the masses whom Hitler in fact despised. Their natural instinct, he believed, was to follow the dictates of their leader who manifested their true will. This was only dissipated in democracy, which undermines the will to act, and destroys unity of purpose. In contrast, whatever conduces to strength, unity and action is good, and in practice Hitler took traditional military organization as his model. Hence the development of the *Fueherprinzip*, or 'leadership-principle', which was first applied to the organization of the Party, and, after 1933, to the government of the state. The function of the Fuehrer in the Party is made clear in Hitler's own words:

'The official in charge . . . listens to various expressions of opinion and then on his side gives his decision. There is no decision possible for which one man does not assume responsibility. That is the ruling principle of our movement.'

Theoretically the Fuehrer was held to be the personification of the spirit of the *Volk*, which may lie dormant, or be mislead, for centuries, but is eventually made manifest in the person of its leader. Thus Dr. Hans Frank, a leading Nazi lawyer, could write in the *Voelkischer Beobachter* in 1936: 'Our constitution is the will of the Fuehrer.' No rational justification for such assertions was ever thought necessary by the Nazis, who accepted the mystical concept of their leader as being the incarnation of the unity of the *Volk*. Hitler clearly felt, with some justification, that his power was more firmly rooted in the people than that of the Kaisers had been between 1871 and 1918.

The *Fueherprinzip* reflected Hitler's belief that the great events and achievements of history are the work of great men, although in some circumstances the credit for these might be extended to an aristocratic group or élite. The role of the élite was fulfilled, in the work of Nazism, by the Party. The latter was no more a party, in the usual English sense of the word, than is the Communist Party. It was not a collection of supporters but an elect body, disciplined, and with specific functions. It acted as a link between the Fuehrer and the *Volk*, so that Hitler was able to deny, at least to his own satisfaction, that he was a dictator. Further, the education of the *Volk* in the Nazi *weltanschauung* was its responsibility, although 'educate' is too mild a verb to describe the ruthless techniques the élite brought to its ordained task.

An adjunct to the idea of the racial folk was that of *Lebensraum*, or living space. It was elaborated from ideas that had long been current in Europe, and, fundamentally, envisaged a powerful Germany in Central and Eastern Europe, expanding as far as military power would permit. Rudolf Kjellén, a Swedish political theorist, had expanded the plan into a philosophy which he called *Geopolitik*, and it was under this name that the Nazis, particularly Karl Haushofer, popularized it.

The distinctive element of Nazi *geopolitik* was taken from the work of an English geographer, Sir H. J. Mackinder. He had argued that much of Europe's history was explicable in terms of pressure exerted on coastal people by the inhabitants of the landlocked areas in Eastern Europe and Central Asia. 'The Heartland', as he called this area, was the core of the 'World-Island', consisting of Europe, Africa and Asia; Australia and the Americas he regarded as outlying islands. He summarized his own argument thus: 'Who rules East Europe commands the Heartland. Who rules the Heartland commands the World-Island. Who rules the World-Island commands the World.' Mackinder had been advocating a Russian alliance to the statesmen of Edwardian England, but his message seemed equally valid in Germany after 1918. It resolved the conflict between the East Prussian emphasis on land power, and the West German industrialists' emphasis on sea power. Both were important, but territorial expansion to the

East took priority. In practice the problem was Russia; it could be solved either by an alliance in which Germany was the dominant partner, or by conquest.

The pseudo-scientific support given to *geopolitik* was based largely on the concept of struggle. A natural process of selection was held to destroy the weak or non-expanding state. Vigorous states would naturally expand, and fixed frontiers therefore had little significance; they could never be more than the front line of an advancing army. It was mainly as propaganda, to make the Germans 'space-conscious', that these disruptive sentiments were used.

The more effective reasoning behind *geopolitik* lay in Hitler's shrewd appreciation of the primacy of political power over economic prosperity. Economic strength, he argued, rests on political control, and both depend on military strength. Space, as such, was in reality unimportant, but large areas contiguous to Germany, once conquered and effectively controlled, would provide raw materials and other economic requirements in such quantities as to make Germany self-sufficient, a vital factor in a state of war or armed truce. The subject peoples of the conquered regions were destined to serve the master race to maintain its high standard of living, while their own remained perpetually low.

The whole of the Nazi *weltanschauung* brought the movement into conflict with more generous views of life which were painfully seeking roots in the aftermath of the 1914–1918 War. Further struggle was abhorrent to thousands who had fought for no clear purpose except to end conflict, in the mud of Flanders or the heat of Mesopotamia. The League of Nations existed as a possible alternative means of regulating international affairs, although its early attitude in excluding Germany from its councils was notably at variance with its ideals. The injustices of colonialism were being challenged in India, but the equality of nations was clearly not compatible with the racial theories of *The Myth of the Twentieth Century*, while the whole complex of *Volk*, élite, and Fuehrer, was inimical to democracy. Also it was implacably hostile to Marxism, for the theory of inevitable class war was cut sharply across the image of the closely knit *Volk*. This was to be of some significance later, when tolerance of Nazism was rationalized on the grounds that it served as a barrier between Communism and Western Europe. *Geopolitik* clearly invalidated international law, or agreements, in the minds of those who believed in it. At best they could never be more than uneasy lulls in a state of incessant conflict.

Everything the Nazis hated was symbolized for them by the Jews. Their anti-semitism was deeply felt, and was to be borne out in pogroms of unequalled ferocity. The repetitive pages of *Mein Kampf* are filled with such denunciations of the Jews as to be evidence of a diseased mind. Hitler saw them as the pillars of democracy, the agents of Marxism, the leaders of trade unions, and the speculators behind international finance. They were intent on adulterating the racial purity of the German people, and they advocated the use of Esperanto to destroy pride in native language. At times this irrational loathing spills over into obscene raving :

'The Jew is . . . a parasite, a sponger . . . a pernicious bacillus . . . his presence is also like that of a vampire; for wherever he establishes himself the people . . . are bound to be bled to death. . . .'

To argue that these ideas won favour in Germany because the Germans suffer a certain lack of intellectual perception would be to concede some possibility of truth in racial theory. Why they did so on such a scale is in part explained by post-war social and economic conditions which will be considered later. But part of the explanation lies in an intellectual climate of opinion which had existed before the war, and may have been intensified by the bewilderment of defeat.

The name National-Socialism summarized an idea, which was old and familiar, that the nation's resources might be consolidated for national purposes. A good deal of nineteenth-century socialist speculation in Germany had deviated from Marxism in supplanting internationalism by state socialism, and the class struggle by co-operation between capital and labour. Oswald Spengler revived this idea after 1918. He, too, saw the world in terms of struggle and racial conflict, and argued that socialism should be purged of internationalism and the class war, and what remained incorporated with Prussian traditions of discipline and authority. His concept of society included a landowner-industrialist class, a rural economy based on peasant husbandry, sufficient industry to provide adequate military strength, and a disciplined working class. Such a programme had obvious attractions for the Junkers and industrialists; in addition it has been suggested that Nazi propaganda attracted the working class to it by using the nation as a utopian replacement for the classless society.

Racialism too, as has already been suggested, had been expressed in various forms for decades prior to 1914. Virulent anti-semitism had been a social disease in Central Europe for centuries; indeed the Jew-badge, and body tax, required of all Jews in the Habsburg lands before the eighteenth century reforms of Joseph II, were precursors of Nazi methods. It was relatively simple for demagogues to exploit this irrational hatred.

The cult of the *Volk* had been strong in German literary romanticism as early as the eighteenth century, when Herder favourably contrasted 'genuine folk thought' with French rationalism. Romanticism tended also to exalt the hero figure who from time to time emerged from the soul of the *Volk* to perform deeds of great valour. Even further back lay the legend of the *heimliche Kaiser*, the hidden Emperor, Frederick Barbarossa, the greatest ruler of the Medieval Empire. That he lay sleeping, and would return when Germany lay stricken, to lead her back to glory, was a pagan tradition still not dead. In 1925 Carl Burckhardt, the Swiss historian, wrote to a friend, telling him of a meeting with an old acquaintance from his student days at Göttingen University. This man, in his middle thirties, had spoken with grim fanaticism of the coming of the *heimliche Kaiser*, who would remove all traces of Western decadence from the German people.

Lebensraum had obvious appeal for the supporters of Pan-Germanism. Before 1914 it was widely felt that the Austrian Empire had sacrificed the interests of the German people to the dynastic interests of the Habsburgs. The latter had accepted the Magyars as virtually equal partners in 1867, and seemed unlikely to hold out much longer against the demands of the Slav peoples within their boundaries. The historical memory of the Medieval Empire in the heyday of the Hohenstaufen dynasty had always been attractive, and the programme of George von Schoenerer's Pan-German Nationalists attracted many, including Adolf Hitler, in Vienna before the Great War.

Finally, the very irrationalism of Nazi arguments had irresistible appeal. It absolved many from the hard responsibility of thinking, and it chimed closely with an existing school of thought.

Early opponents of the movement described it as a 'revolt against reason', and the Nazis prided themselves that this was so. They frequently asserted that life controls reason, that great deeds are the product not of intelligence, but the heroic will, and that people are preserved and flourish through a racial intuition. Liberalism and Marxism alike were swept aside contemptuously as products of rational thought.

Irrationalism had been a persistent strand in nineteenth-century thought. In origin it probably reflected disillusionment with industrial society, for it was most popular among artists and mystics for whom such a society was seldom congenial. Arthur Schopenhauer and Friedrich Nietzsche were the outstanding figures in this school of thought. The former saw what he called 'will' acting behind all human life. The struggle of this force was incessant and without meaning. It could create and destroy, but never attain its goal, for it could be satisfied with nothing. Amid this confusion the seeming reasonableness established by the human mind is only apparent. Thus all achievement is illusory and Schopenhauer saw some form of spiritual asceticism as the only hope for mankind. Nietzsche accepted Schopenhauer's 'will', but argued that if achievement really means only man's urge to strive, then man should accept the struggle joyfully. Clearly this was no philosophy for the masses whose role was to follow the heroic figure of their leader through the conflict that was life.

More closely associated with science was a second strand of irrationalism. It derived from the biological discoveries that reason has a naturalistic origin in organic evolution, and that scientific method included the use of assumptions which are not rationally apparent but could be used as conventions on which to base further experiment.

Henry Bergson, a Frenchman, combined the two strands. He purported to show that intelligence is the servant of the 'life-force', an obscure element like Schopenhauer's 'will'. Only intuition, Bergson claimed, can perceive reality. He believed that human beings are well endowed with such intuition, but that it had been suppressed because men depended too much on intelligence.

Irrationalism was first directly applied to society and politics by the French socialist, Georges Sorel, in his *Reflections on Violence*, published in 1908. He sought to discredit Marxism, and used Bergson's 'life-force' to remove from it any theory of social change through rational causes; and he used the concept of intuition to provide a philosophy of revolution. For Sorel, social philosophy became a myth, which concept he never completely defined. In effect it was a kind of vision which would inspire the followers of a cause. It was in this sense that Rosenberg used the word myth, and the meaning which Hitler put into *weltanschauung* is virtually the same thing. It is a vision, a view of life, that is completely intolerant of any other, and which fights its opponents ruthlessly and without scruple. Such, in essence, was the idea of Nazism.

CHAPTER TWO

The Fuehrer

ADOLF HITLER is one of the few historical figures whose names have genuinely become household words. Born on 20th April 1889, to obscure lower middle class parents, he died, by his own hand, fifty-six years later, in the burning capital of the Reich he had created.

The role of the Fuehrer was of central importance in the Nazi movement. Without Hitler Nazism would not have become the force it did, and some knowledge of his character and formative years is essential to an understanding of the movement he led.

His ancestry and early years were once obscured by the misleading autobiographical information in *Mein Kampf*, and the blatant hero-worship exuded by his Nazi biographers. Some things remain unknown, but research by Alan Bullock, Franz Jetzinger, and others, has made the picture as clear as it is likely to become.

Hitler's paternal grandmother was Maria Anne Shickelgruber, who bore an illegitimate son, Alois, in 1837. This child was to be the father of Adolf Hitler. It was once assumed that Alois's father was Johann Heidler who married Maria Shickelgruber in 1842. In 1876, long after both parents were dead, the relevant entry in the parish register at Dollersheim was amended to legitimatize Alois as Hiedler, or Hitler as he chose to call himself. In fact the alteration was probably a put-up job, engineered by Nepomuk Hiedler, brother of the putative father, who had taken Alois into his home, after the mother's death, and probably wished to further his career. Thus Hitler's ancestry remains unclear. It is possible that his paternal grandfather was the son of his grandmother's one-time employers, the Frankenberger family of Graz. Ironically, the Frankenbergers were Jews.

Long before he was legitimatized, Alois Shickelgruber worked hard to climb the promotion ladders, first of the Austrian border police, and then the customs service. He resigned from the latter in 1895, having reached the highest rank open to one of his limited education, and lived in retirement until 1903. This man, one of the earliest influences on Adolf Hitler, appears then to have been a conscientious official. But there are clear signs of instability. He married three times and was separated once. One wife was eleven years older than he, and the third, Adolf's mother, twenty-three years younger. He sired eight children, of whom three were conceived out of wedlock. As a father he may have been hard and unsympathetic, but his obituary, in the *Linzer Tagespost*, suggests that he was a popular man in the district, although hot-tempered. In all he was probably a typical late nineteenth century paterfamilias, and the conflicts between him and his son, largely the fault of the latter.

For the first six years of his life, while his father was still a serving official, Adolf lived with his parents, first at Branau and then at Passau. On retirement the father bought a smallholding at Fischlhalm where Adolf attended the village school. After selling the smallholding, the family moved to Lambach, where Adolf attended the elementary school and finally settled near Linz, where Adolf attended both the elementary and the commercial-technical schools, leaving in 1905. For the next two years he was completely idle, and when he inherited his share of his father's will he moved to Vienna. The first stage of his life was over.

In these early years he was materially comfortable. At the time of his birth his father's salary was higher than that of the headmaster of an Austrian secondary school; he retired on half-pay, and an adequate pension was paid to his family upon his death. That the Hitlers were left reasonably well off is suggested by the fact that Adolf lived without working for two years after he left school. The poverty he later endured was entirely his own fault.

Jetzinger attaches considerable psychological importance to the years spent at Passau, where Hitler was in contact with the more nationalist children of South Bavaria, who celebrated the *Sedanfeier*, the anniversary of the German victory over France in 1871. The teacher at Fischlhalm village school remembered him as lively, intelligent, and well turned out, but his record at the commercial-technical school was uniformly bad. He was obliged to repeat his first year's work there and his teachers agreed that, although he was not untalented, he was remarkably idle. In later life Hitler was contemptuous of education and the only one of his teachers he remembered favourably was one Dr. Poetsch, whose history lessons appear to have been rabid nationalist propaganda. The Nazi view, that Hitler's record at school was largely due to illness, may be discounted. It also seems likely that it was his failure there that occasioned the quarrel with his father that Hitler described in *Mein Kampf*. According to this version Hitler's father opposed his son's ambition to embark on a career in art, insisting that he should enter the customs service.

Certainly some major disturbance affected Hitler at the time of puberty. He was a pleasant child but an entirely different adolescent. He became pale, almost tubercular in appearance, solitary and without friends, opinionated, rebellious and given to fantasy. None of these symptoms is abnormal in adolescence, but in Hitler they took an extreme form, and he never outgrew them. At this crucial stage he lost his father, and his mother clearly doted on him, indulging every whim. Between 1905 and 1908 Hitler came nearer than he ever did again to forming a friendship, with one Augustus Kubizek. The latter, younger and an intellectual lightweight, appears to have served as an audience to whom Hitler poured out his immature views on art and life. No political consciousness had as yet developed.

In April 1907, at the age of eighteen, Hitler inherited a share of his father's will, estimated at 200 crowns, and moved to Vienna, where he failed to gain entrance to the Academy of Arts. He returned to Linz on his mother's death, stayed long enough to secure an orphan's pension, on the grounds that he was a student, and returned to Vienna taking Kubizek with him. While his money lasted he did nothing, but by the end of 1908 his small capital was spent, he had broken with Kubizek, and again failed to enter the Academy of Arts or the School of Architecture.

In the summer of 1909 he slept on park benches, and during the winter took refuge in an Asylum for the Homeless where he became acquainted with a tramp, Reinhold Hanisch. For a year they were partners, Hitler painting postcard scenes of Vienna, and Hanisch peddling them in the streets. The partnership ended when Hitler brought a lawsuit against Hanisch for swindling, and got him one week's imprisonment. From then until 1914 he eked out an existence in Vienna, and later, Munich, painting cheap postcards and advertisements for small shops. In 1911 the authorities, not unreasonably, deprived him of the orphan's pension, and in 1913 he moved to Munich to avoid conscription into the Habsburg army. Eventually the Austrian authorities obliged him to report for medical examination, but, on failing this, he was rejected for military service. He was still in Munich in 1914 and, on the declaration of war, volunteered, and was accepted, for service in a Bavarian infantry regiment.

It may be supposed that Hitler's appearance was seldom prepossessing in the days when he chose to live as a down and out. In 1910, according to Hanisch, his face was thin with staring eyes, he had an unkempt black beard, his hair was long and over his coat collar, and he wore ill-fitting secondhand clothes. He was, said Hanisch, 'an apparition such as rarely occurs among Christians'. He was lazy and moody, characteristics which recurred throughout his life. He neither smoked nor drank, and seems to have been unattracted by women. At times he was seized with enthusiasm for a new invention, or some obscure branch of learning, but his interest soon flagged. Clearly it was during this time that he developed a passion for politics, and this did not flag. He went for days on end, hanging about doss-houses, discussing politics and frequently losing his temper. The power of the spoken word also captured his imagination, and Hanisch told how Hitler went to a cinema — he was to remain an inveterate cinema goer — to see Kellermann's 'Tunnel'. In this an agitator appeared who roused the masses by his oratory, and for days afterwards Hitler spoke of nothing else.

The ideas that Hitler accumulated in Vienna have in part been considered. Struggle was the normal philosophy in his social world. Among men living on the fringe of the law, in constant fear of the police or their own pasts, disloyalty and dishonesty were commonplace. Throughout his life, Hitler showed no loyalty to his associates, and an unscrupulousness that appalled men who prided themselves on their own lack of scruple. He was an accomplished liar, and believed that men's motives are invariably ignoble.

He came to perceive how people can be manipulated both as individuals, and in the mass by playing on their weaknesses. Not long before coming to power he averred, in private conversation, that the masses want only 'bread and circuses', and it was in Vienna that he developed this contempt for working men. He hated the social democratic politicians and trade union leaders, who preached equality and working class solidarity, and their whole ideology was alien to him. The hopes and fears of the lower middle class also impressed him. Here were people of narrow outlook, preoccupied with their sense of respectability, eager to conform, ready to accept uncritically any leader who preserved their material interests, contemptuous of those lower in the social scale, and fearful of descent to that level. Hitler never lost his awareness of such folk, and they flocked to him in the nineteen-thirties.

Democratic institutions also earned his dislike during his time in Vienna, and his views on them, previously outlined, date from that time. It was also here that his distaste for notions of racial equality developed. Hitler was horrified by the failure of the Germans in the Habsburg Empire to subject its Slav population. He began to dream of a united Greater Reich, a dream that he was to make real when the opportunity arose in 1938.

It was in the Austrian capital that the seeds of the 'Final Solution' were sown. There was nothing original in Hitler's

opinion of the Jews. Anti-semitism was endemic in Vienna, and
everything he ever wrote about the Jews was commonplace in
the anti-semitic newspapers and pamphlets he read there before
1914. Viennese anti-semitism was marked by its sexuality, and
Hitler wrote in *Mein Kampf* of 'the nightmare vision of the
seduction of thousands of girls by repulsive, crooked-legged Jew
bastards'. It has been suggested that an unfortunate sexual experience, perhaps the contraction of venereal disease, was at the
root of Hitler's anti-semitism. Whatever the root cause, it was to
be of dreadful significance in Europe.

Finally, although he played no active part in politics before
1914, Hitler seems to have learned a good deal, by observation,
of political tactics. In particular he learned how to create a mass
movement, and how to win power on the basis of the random
ideas he had picked up. The three parties who unknowingly
taught him these lessons were the Austrian Social Democrats,
Georg von Schoenerer's Pan-German Nationalists, and Karl
Lueger's Christian Social Party.

Although he despised the Social Democrats, Hitler was impressed by them and the power of a mass party and mass propaganda. He wrote in *Mein Kampf* :

'. . . The masses of the people prefer the ruler to the suppliant
and are filled with a stronger sense of mental security by a teaching that brooks no rival than by a teaching that offers them a
liberal choice. They have very little idea of how to make such a
choice and . . . feel . . . abandoned . . . they feel very little
shame at being terrorized intellectually and are scarcely conscious
that their freedom . . . is . . . abused . . . also, physical intimidation has its significance for the masses as well as the
individual.'

From the Pan-German Nationalists he learned what not to do.
They failed, Hitler thought, by neglecting the masses, wasting
their energies in parliamentary conflict, and splitting their potential support by gratuitous attacks on the Church. Again in *Mein
Kampf* he wrote :

'The art of leadership consists of consolidating the attention of the people against a single adversary and taking care that nothing will split up this attention. . . . The leader of genius must have the ability to make different opponents appear as if they belonged to one category.'

In Karl Lueger, leader of the Christian Social Party, Hitler saw the success of the tactics that Schoenerer neglected. His strength lay in the support of the Viennese lower middle class. He also made an ally of the Church, and, in a most significant passage, Hitler commented:

'He was quick to adopt all available means for winning the support of long-established institutions, so as to be able to derive the greatest possible advantage for his movement from those old sources of power.'

Hitler compared Schoenerer's and Lueger's leadership thus:

'If the Christian Social Party, together with its shrewd judgment in regard to the worth of the popular masses, had only judged rightly also on the importance of the racial problem — which was properly grasped by the Pan-German movement — and if this party had been really nationalist; or if the Pan-German leaders on the other hand, in addition to their correct judgment of the Jewish problem and of the national idea, had adopted the practical wisdom of the Christian-Social Party, and particularly their attitude towards Socialism — then a movement would have developed which might have successfully altered the course of German destiny.'

This was already the idea of a party which should be both nationalist and socialist. The words were written some years after Hitler left Vienna, and it is not to be supposed that his ideas were so clearly formulated before 1914. But the years between were a time of gestation, and of his time in Vienna Hitler truthfully remarked:

'During these years a view of life . . . took shape in my mind . . . I have changed nothing in it . . . Vienna . . . taught me the most profound lessons of my life.'

Why Hitler should have volunteered as a soldier in 1914 is not immediately clear, and his early years do not suggest that a closely regulated life would have appealed to him. Probably his nationalist ardour, the opportunity to escape from his failures, and the war hysteria which swept Europe, all played their part. He was prepared for the first time, to take orders, lead a disciplined existence, and do a job of work.

He served in the List Regiment, and seems to have been an exemplary soldier. He acted as a runner between the front and regimental headquarters, moving along communication lines which were often subject to shell fire. He was awarded the coveted Iron Cross, but the circumstances of this are unknown. He was wounded in 1916, promoted to lance-corporal in the following year, gassed in 1918, and was still temporarily blind and in hospital when the war ended.

It is curious, in the circumstances, that Hitler won so little promotion. Indeed he might well have been expected to be granted a commission in view of the German officer shortage at the end of the war. His eccentricity may have hindered him; certainly he was thought odd by his comrades, although they did not dislike him. At times he spoke to no one, and at others launched himself into an anti-semitic harangue without any provocation other than his own train of thought. He apparently had no contacts at home, cared nothing for leave, and did not join in the endless grumbles about army life. It is probably true that Hitler found war, for all its dangers and discomforts, an exhilarating experience in contrast to civilian life. Not that he was unique in this respect; there were unsettled ex-soldiers throughout Europe after the war, and some of those in Germany were among Nazism's first recruits. Again, like most men in all the armies involved in the Great War, Hitler was understandably contemptuous of those who evaded military service, the black-marketeers, the politicians and the journalists. But Hitler labelled them all as Jews, and Nazi propaganda made the Jews responsible for the defeat of the German army.

Undoubtedly defeat came as a tremendous shock to Hitler. Having recovered from it he determined, according to his own version, to enter politics. His course, he claimed later, had become clear to him. This was probably no more than a rationalization of what happened later, although there is no denying his interest in politics.

When his sight returned Hitler was discharged from Pasewalk military hospital and rejoined his regiment in Munich, where he acted as a prison camp guard until January 1919. By then his political views had come to the notice of his superiors. He had been selected to attend a course of army lectures, organized for the purpose of political indoctrination. During a discussion someone defended the Jews and Hitler spoke vigorously in reply. His impeccable sentiments were noted by his commanding officer, Major Giehrl, and he was seconded as an instruction officer to the Press and News Bureau of the Political Department of the German Army's Munich District Command. His task was to indoctrinate men against socialism, pacifism and democracy, which Hitler and the German Army crudely regarded as indistinguishable.

In September 1919 he was ordered to investigate a small group calling itself the German Workers Party. This was the seed he was to nourish into the Nazi movement. Following his intervention at the meeting he had been ordered to attend, Hitler was invited to join the committee, and quickly became its outstanding member. He was demobilized in 1920 and became a full-time political worker. In July 1921 a conflict between him and other committee members ended in his being given dictatorial powers in the party. Thus was established the leadership principle, the first law of the Nazi Party and, later, of the Third Reich. The Fuehrer had arrived in German politics.

CHAPTER THREE

The Elite

WHEN Hitler first met the German Workers Party on 12th September 1919, in a dingy Munich beer hall, the Sternukerbrau, it had some fifty adherents. By 1931 membership totalled over 800,000, and its para-military wing was four times the size of the German army.

The Party was founded in 1918 by Anton Drexler, a Munich locksmith, when he organized a Committee of Independent Workmen to combat Marxism in the trade union movement; in 1919 he merged it with a similar body led by a journalist, Karl Harrer. It aimed to harness working-class support to a nationalist movement which would focus German resentment on the Versailles Peace Treaty.

It was not unique or original. In Bavaria itself similar groups were led by Julius Streicher in Nuremberg and Otto Dickel in Augsburg. In Austria there had been several attempts to form such a party, even before the war. The most successful, led by Walther Riehl, a lawyer, and Rudolf Jung, a railway employee, formulated a strongly nationalist, anti-semitic programme, and in 1918 adopted the title of German National Socialist Workers Party, with branches in Vienna and the Sudetenland, in Czechoslovakia. For a time there were contacts with Bavaria, but these were insignificant, and ended in 1923. Nazism remained active in Austria and the Sudetenland, but its mainstream was in Germany.

Hitler quickly dominated the party committee. He organized larger meetings, inserting notices of them in the press and getting invitations mimeographed. During 1920 the name of National Socialist German Workers Party was adopted and, with it, an official programme. This demanded the union of all German people to form a Great Germany (in contrast to the Little Germany created by Bismarck in 1871), the abolition of the Versailles Treaty, and the cession of 'colonies' to Germany to allow for population expansion. Citizens of the state were to be equal, but only those of German blood could be citizens, enjoying political rights and official appointments. The first duty of all citizens was to work for the good of the state, and education was to be made available to all, but its prime function was to teach state sociology. Standards of public health were to be raised by measures protecting mothers and children, and by making gymnastics obligatory. Freedom of the press, and Christianity, were to be permitted within a framework conducive to the national welfare, and acceptable to the moral sense of the German race. Aliens were to enjoy few rights, and Jews, in particular, were to be discriminated against. A national army was to be formed, and Article 16, aimed at the lower middle class, emphasized the need to strengthen that section of the community. Socialist measures included abolition of unearned income, confiscation of war profits, nationalization of Trusts, profit-sharing in industry, provision for old age, land reform, and the death-penalty for profiteers. Finally, a strong central authority was to be erected, parliamentary in form, although the programme implied strong criticism of the parliamentary system. That this was catchpenny propaganda is clear, but it was declared unalterable and a good deal of it was eventually fulfilled.

The *fuehrerprinzip* was established in the summer of 1921. During Hitler's absence in North Germany, where he was contacting other nationalist elements, a group in the Munich committee challenged his claims to leadership. Returning to Bavaria, Hitler offered his resignation which the committee rejected, not wishing to lose its most able speaker and fund-raiser, whereupon Hitler demanded that absolute power be vested in him. At first the committee fought, circulating a pamphlet indicting his 'im-

PLATE I. Brownshirts attempting to rally support in their early days. It must have been easy for most Germans to dismiss them as insignificant.

moral purposes', but Hitler sued the authors for libel and Drexler was obliged to repudiate it. Opposition collapsed, and the party statutes were altered to give Hitler dictatorial powers as president.

Meanwhile, in 1920, the 'Gymnastic and Sports Division' of the party was organized. Originally consisting of gangs of thugs, led by an ex-convict, Emil Maurice, it was renamed, in October 1921, the *Sturmabteilung*, the S.A. Members wore brown uniforms, and their functions were to maintain order at Nazi meetings and disrupt those of their opponents. Hitler served one month in prison during 1921 after leading an S.A. attack on a political rally.

The party flag, bearing the swastika, was adopted. Its red background indicated the social idea of the movement, the white circle its nationalism, and the swastika its 'mission of struggle for the victory of Aryan man'. The swastika is of ancient origin, having been found in the ruins of Troy, Greece, India and China. Certain Freikorps* units wore it, and the Austrian national socialists adopted it, but it was the German Nazis who were to make it a symbol of terror throughout Europe. Later, Hitler designed the Nazi standards which were carried at party rallies. Based on those carried by the Roman legions, they consisted of a black metal swastika on top with a silver wreath surmounted by an eagle, and, below, the initials N.S.D.A.P. on a metal rectangle from which hung cords with fringe and tassels, and a square swastika flag bearing the legend 'Deutschland Erwache!' The significance of such items is not to be underrated. Dramatic symbols and insignia have a powerful effect on men's minds. Napoleon instituted the Legion of Honour because he believed that mankind could be governed by baubles.

In December 1920 the party bought a declining anti-semitic newspaper, the *Voelkischer Beobachter*, a prerequisite for spreading propaganda in Germany, where all important political parties had their own journal. Published weekly at first, it became a daily in 1923.

Permanent offices were opened at 12 Corneliusstrasse in

* See p. 26.

B

Munich, and office furniture, files, a typewriter, telephone and paid secretary gradually acquired.

Clearly this cost a great deal of money. Members' subscriptions, collections taken at meetings, Hitler's fees as a speaker for other bodies, and the royalties from *Mein Kampf* were a drop in the ocean. The army helped to buy the *Voelkischer Beobachter*. Ernst Roehm, organizer of the S.A., but still a *Reichswehr* officer, persuaded General Ritter von Epp, another party member, to contribute some of the 60,000 marks required, and a proportion of it came from army secret funds. The army also provided the S.A. with sidearms, lent them rifles, gave them tactical and weapons training and allowed them to take part in manoeuvres.

Some party members, like Dietricht Eckart and Hermann Goering, were affluent and made considerable financial contributions. Eckart found half the money to buy the *Voelkischer Beobachter*, and introduced Hitler to moneyed and influential circles. The Bechsteins, wealthy piano manufacturers, were among these; Helene Bechstein gave parties for her friends to meet Hitler, and raised money for the party. Ernst Hanfstaengl, whose family owned an art publishing business, loaned the party 1000 dollars against a mortgage on the *Voelkischer Beobachter*, an astronomical sum in the inflationary days of 1923. Gertrud von Seydlitz, who owned stock in Finnish paper mills, contributed; Hermann Aust, a businessman, collected gifts after Hitler had addressed the Herrenklub in Munich; and one Dr. Gansser put Hitler in touch with a number of Berlin businessmen. Occasionally lavish donations were received, for example Fritz Thyssen of United Steel gave 100,000 gold marks in 1923.

Rumours that Nazism was financed by the French have not been proven, but it is possible that money came from Switzerland. Altogether the movement was launched on slender resources and a tiny guaranteed income.

The Party grew in strength to about 20,000 members. In general terms it is clear who these people were. Undoubtedly it was from the *Freikorps* that many of the S.A. were recruited. These were armed bands of freebooters that came into existence at the end of the war. The army used them to defend the eastern frontier against Poland, and they were employed, with the government's consent, to suppress the Spartakist risings of 1918–1919. After 1920 they were obliged to disband, and many of their number were to be found in Bavaria, which was a hotbed of disloyalty to the new Republican government in Berlin. They were men who, in retrospect at least, had enjoyed war, and many had known no other adult occupation. For over four years their readiness to fight had been a virtue, but 1918 saw a return to civilian standards. Maladjusted men of this kind were common throughout Europe. The English government had no difficulty in recruiting the 'Black and Tans' whose indiscipline became notorious during the Irish troubles in the early nineteen twenties.

Nazism's propaganda attracted all who were dissatisfied. Ex-officers like Hess, their status gone, embittered intellectuals like Rosenberg, small shopkeepers who hated Jewish-controlled chain stores, indeed anyone with a grievance, often as much imagined as real, was attracted to the party.

These were the genuine believers, who subscribed to Nazism long before there was pressure on them to do so, and they were but a small proportion of the German population. It should be emphasized that the majority of Germans were not, in this sense, Nazis. Certainly the majority came to accept Nazism, but the circumstances which led millions to vote for the Party, and thousands to join its ranks, will be considered later. The Nazi élite have been described with complete justification as 'murderers, pimps, homosexual perverts, drug addicts or just plain rowdies'.*

Although he founded the Party, Anton Drexler was a nonentity. A sickly bespectacled locksmith of little education, he represented the bigoted lower middle class mind which was attracted to the Nazis. After his clash with Hitler in 1921 his star faded. He left the Party in 1923, and although reconciled in 1930 never returned to active politics.

Dietrich Eckart was a journalist and a poet and dramatist of

* *The Rise and Fall of the Third Reich* by W. L. Shirer (Secker and Warburg, 1960).

sorts, a drunkard and a drug addict, he may have been certified at one time. His services to Nazism ended in 1923 when he expired from heavy drinking. Ernst Roehm was a professional soldier of humble origins and a notorious homosexual. As a staff captain he had invaluable contacts with the army, and was leading organizer of the S.A. One of the few Nazis prepared openly to challenge Hitler, he saw the S.A. as a 'hidden' military force which could one day absorb the *Reichswehr*, whereas Hitler intended to keep it as a subordinate wing of the Party. Hence Roehm's murder in 1934.

Alfred Rosenberg was of Baltic-German stock, born in Estonia and the son of a shoemaker. His Diploma in Architecture from Moscow University may have impressed Hitler, and he was regarded as an intellectual. Hopelessly inept as a politician, he served the movement in various capacities including editing the *Voelkischer Beobachter*.

Gottfried Feder was an engineer, and crank economist. An original party member, he helped to draw up its programme and hoped to implement its socialist points as late as 1933.

Hermann Goering had commanded the famous Richthofen fighter squadron during the war, and held the Pour le Mérite. After the war he married a wealthy Swedish divorcée, and dabbled at Munich University. In addition to helping the Party financially, he helped Roehm to organize the S.A.

Rudolf Hess was the son of a German wholesale merchant in Egypt, where he had lived for some years. During the war he had served, like Hitler, in the List Regiment and, later, as a pilot. After the war he became a student at Munich, where he joined the Party. He was a bitter anti-semitic, and introduced Hitler to geopolitics. Nearly to the end he remained one of the Fuehrer's most loyal followers, and was one of the few Nazi leaders not consumed by personal ambition.

Julius Streicher was a school-teacher, a sadist who invariably carried a whip, and a pornographer who led a blatantly promiscuous life. He led an early 'nazi' group in Nuremberg, but Hitler persuaded him to join the main Party. He ran *Der Stuermer*, an obscene anti-semitic weekly, and remained a leading Nazi until 1939, after when his influence waned. The business manager of the Party and its newspaper was Max Amman. Typical of the lesser lights were Emil Maurice, Christian Weber, a notorious brawler, Max Hoffman, Hitler's valet, and Ulrich Graf, an amateur wrestler and the Fuehrer's bodyguard. Already in the Party by 1923, but not yet prominent, were Gregor Strasser, Joseph Goebbels, and Heinrich Himmler.

By 1923 the Nazi Party was unknown outside Bavaria, and, even there, was not the outstanding political group. It was nevertheless in 1923 that the Nazis made their first bid for power, the Beer Hall *Putsch*.

Circumstances seemed propitious. The Weimar Constitution of 1919 was proving difficult to work, powerful interests like the industrialists were hostile to it, and the Versailles Treaty was universally disliked. Inflation reached a climax in 1923 when the mark collapsed, while early in the year France reoccupied the Ruhr to enforce reparation payments. This factor militated against the Nazis. Hitler's intention was to overthrow the 'November Criminals', as he habitually described the Berlin government which had surrendered to the allies in November 1918, while French policy was rallying the country behind it. Immersed in the Bavarian atmosphere, where hostility to Berlin was rife, Hitler misjudged the situation and made vague plans to march on the capital hoping for support from other dissident groups. Possibly he was aping Mussolini's successful march on Rome of the previous year.

In September 1923 the Chancellor, Gustav Stresemann, adopted the wise but unpopular policies of ending passive resistance in the Ruhr, and resuming reparation payments. Immediately the government was harassed on all sides. In Saxony and the Ruhr, Communist risings seemed likely, a separatist movement flourished in the Rhineland, and in the North the Black Reichswehr, a para-military organization under a Major Buchrucker, attempted revolt, and in Bavaria the *Deutscher Kampfbund*, an alliance of nationalist parties, came into existence. Indeed the

Bavarian State Government itself was on the brink of secession. It declared a state of emergency, nominating Gustav von Kahr as State Commissioner, with dictatorial powers. He was aided by Otto von Lossow, Commanding Officer of the *Reichswehr* in Bavaria, and Hans von Seisser, head of the state police, and the triumvirate declined to acknowledge orders from Berlin, for example Lossow's replacement by General von Kressenstein.

Meanwhile the Reich government had placed full executive power in the hands of Otto Gessler, the defence minister, so that practical responsibility for dealing with the crisis rested with Hans von Seeckt, Commander in Chief of the *Reichswehr*. Having crushed the Communist insurgents, Seeckt made it clear that he would do the same to the Bavarians. Faced with the might of the army the triumvirate lost heart, and Hitler realized that, without their support, his cause was in jeopardy.

At the instigation of Alfred Rosenberg, and Max Erwin von Scheubner-Richter, another Baltic-German of doubtful repute, Hitler determined to kidnap the triumvirate and force it to exercise authority on his behalf. One attempt to do so was abortive, and another planned, but, in the event, an impromptu scheme was put into operation on 8th November.

It was announced in the press that on that evening Kahr, accompanied by his associates, would address a public meeting at the Buergerbraükeller on the outskirts of Munich. Hitler was convinced that Kahr would announce Bavarian secession and the restoration of the Wittelsbach monarchy, which he was known to favour.

Shortly after the meeting began the S.A. surrounded the building. Hitler walked in, fired a pistol to draw attention to himself, and herded the triumvirate into a side room at gun point, leaving Goering to exhort the astonished audience to remain calm and drink its beer. The triumvirate refused to meet Hitler's demands so he locked them in and returned to the main hall, where he declared that they had formed a provisional Reich government with him. The applause which greeted this mendacious statement temporarily impressed the triumvirate. Meanwhile, a messenger had brought to the scene General Ludendorff, one of Germany's great war heroes, who now lived in Bavaria and was active in anti-Republican politics. Ludendorff was outraged by Hitler's precipitate action but, with complete lack of political acumen, advised the triumvirate to co-operate. Returning to the platform the five men publicly swore loyalty to each other and their new régime, whereupon the meeting broke up.

At this juncture Hitler was called away from the Hall, and returned to find the triumvirate gone. Kahr had promptly moved his seat of government to Regensburg, leaving orders for Munich to be posted with notices denouncing the *putsch*. During the confused night that followed, it became clear that neither the local *Reichswehr* units nor the police would desert to the Nazis, although no attempt was made to disarm the S.A. in the Buergerbraükeller gardens. When morning came, Ludendorff proposed that they should march into the centre of the city and take it over, being convinced that neither soldiers nor police would fire on such a legendary figure as he. Lacking a better plan, Hitler agreed.

The Nazi column bluffed its way past one armed police unit, but found its way barred where the narrow Residenzstrasse opened out into the Odeonsplatz. Which side fired first is not clear, but, as a fusillade of shots rang out, the Nazis broke and fled, none taking more briskly to his heels than the Fuehrer, who was driven away, in a waiting car, to the country home of the Hanfstaengls, where he was arrested two days later.

The trial of the conspirators throws a discreditable light on the administration of justice in Weimar Germany. The influence of Franz Guertner, Bavarian Minister of Justice, ensured that the bench would be tolerant, and Hitler was allowed to interrupt or cross-examine witnesses almost at will. Although there were others on trial, it was the Fuehrer who stole the limelight. Arrogantly, he asserted that he had committed no crime, that the Republican government which had surrendered to the Allies in 1918 was the true criminal, and that his *putsch* was a justifiable attempt to restore German honour. Whatever judgment the court passed, he said, history would acquit him. Absurdly lenient sentences were passed, Ludendorff being acquitted, and Hitler receiving five years' imprisonment, with the assurance that he would be eligible for parole in six months.

Hitler was confined in the Landsberg Fortress Prison, where he lived, with certain of his associates, in considerable comfort, and began to dictate *Mein Kampf*, although it was not finished until after his release. The Nazi Party was proscribed and its press barred throughout the Reich. In his absence Hitler appointed Rosenberg to lead the movement, and it became torn by internecine strife. At the Reichstag elections of May 1924 the Nazis combined with other similar groups to win thirty-two seats, but this number dropped to fourteen in December. In contrast the Republic was weathering the storm. Under the direction of Hjalmar Schacht, a financier of outstanding ability, the currency was stabilized, while the Dawes plan eased the reparations burden. The French withdrew from the Ruhr, and Stresemann's policy paved the way for the Locarno Pact and German entry into the League of Nations. American capital began to come into Germany and an era of prosperity opened. When Hitler was paroled in December 1924 Nazism seemed on the verge of extinction.

That it survived was largely due to Hitler. The Fuehrer, still convinced of his destiny, had learned a valuable political lesson. It was clear that armed rebellion was an outdated revolutionary technique. It would be necessary to win power within the framework of the existing constitution and then to use the full power of the state to overthrow it. This was what Hitler meant by the 'policy of legality' which he imposed on the party after his release.

Dressed in this cloak of respectability he encountered little difficulty in persuading the Bavarian State Government to lift its ban, and in February 1925 the Party was reformed and the *Voelkischer Beobachter* reappeared. However, the Fuehrer's tongue soon betrayed him, and his first speech to the Party was so intemperate that he was promptly forbidden to speak in public throughout the Reich. In Prussia the ban lasted until 1928, and it was a serious handicap to a man whose oratory was his main weapon.

The era of prosperity beginning in 1924, and the election of President Hindenburg in 1925, which temporarily reconciled many right wing elements to the Republic, made the Nazi cause a forlorn hope, but Hitler set himself to construct a Party immeasurably more formidable than it had been in 1923. It was created over a number of years, and the following account gives some idea of its complexity when the Nazis came to power in 1933. By then it had become a state within a state.

At its head was Hitler, 'Supreme Leader of the Party and the S.A., Chairman of the National Socialist Labour Organization'. Directly attached to this office was the Reich Directorate, consisting of top men in the Party. Party headquarters were in the Brown House, an old mansion in Munich which was sumptuously refurnished. A grand staircase led up to a conference room furnished in red leather, and a large room where Hitler received visitors beneath a portrait of Frederick the Great, whose contempt for an upstart Austrian corporal can only be imagined.

The country was divided into areas called *Gaue*, an obsolete Germanic word, with racial overtones, which may be translated as 'a subdivision of the tribe'. These corresponded roughly with the thirty-four Reichstag electoral districts, and each was run by a *Gauleiter* appointed by Hitler. They were subdivided into *kreise*, which contained a number of local groups, *ortsgruppen*. The latter were further divided, in large cities into street cells and blocks. Seven additional *Gaue* were established for Austria, Danzig, the Saar, and the Sudetenland.

The Party organization was divided into two main sections. One was directed by Gregor Strasser and designed to undermine the existing state; it had departments for foreign affairs, the press, and the building up of Party cells. Shortly before 1933, as a result of Hitler's feud with Strasser, the section was divided into two with Robert Ley and Goebbels in charge. The second section of party organization was responsible for building a state within a state. Under the direction of Constantin Hierl, it had departments of agriculture, economic policy, race and culture, the interior, legal questions, labour and engineering. In addition Martin Bormann administered a pension fund to assist those killed or disabled in the Party's service.

Propaganda was a separate department which came to be organized by Joseph Goebbels, a genius in this field. He was born of pious working class Catholic parents in the Rhineland, and received a university education. At the age of seven, osteomyelitis made his left leg shorter than his right, and his awareness of this defect may account for his neurotic mind. He was a notorious philanderer, inevitably dissatisfied and frustrated in his emotional life. He was something of a socialist who supported Strasser's first attack on Hitler in 1925, but he was soon reconciled to the Fuehrer, who made him Gauleiter of Berlin and responsible for propaganda.

The character of the Nazis made feuds and intrigue endemic within the Party, and a Party Court, the Uschla, was established to preserve discipline and the authority of the leader. Under Walther Buch, Ulrich Graf, and a young lawyer, Hans Frank, it paid no attention to crime or immorality except in so far as they affected Party unity.

The S.A. got out of control — in September 1930 Goebbels even had to seek the help of the police to evict them from the Berlin Party headquarters which they had smashed up — and Hitler persuaded Roehm to return from Bolivia, where he was serving as a mercenary officer, to reorganize them. He divided Germany into twenty-one districts, with an S.A. group in each commanded by an *Obergruppenfuehrer*. The S.A. had its own H.Q. and General Staff, separate from the Party, and a training college in Munich for its leaders. It had a number of auxiliaries such as the Motor Corps, a flying squad, and by 1932 it numbered 300,000 men.

While the S.A. had been so mutinous Hitler had formed a more dependable body, the *Schutzstaffel*; the S.S. Members wore black uniforms with death's head insignia, and swore an oath of loyalty to Hitler. In 1929 Heinrich Himmler became commander of the S.S. As yet it was little more than Hitler's personal body-guard, and in 1931 was subordinated to Roehm.

Various ancillary organizations were brought into existence. The Hitler Youth took young people from fifteen to eighteen, and the Schoolchildren's League provided for those over ten. Women, students, teachers, civil servants, doctors and lawyers had their separate organizations, while the *Kulturbund* aimed to attract intellectuals and artists.

The cost of running such an organization was astronomical. No detailed accounts are available, but it has been estimated that the S.A. alone cost little under three million marks a week. Hitler himself said that, in the days before he came to power, the bill, when he and his staff stayed at the Kaiserhof in Berlin for a week — as they often did — amounted to 10,000 marks. In addition to normal running expenses, vast sums of money were poured into election campaigns after 1930.

A good deal of the money was raised by the Party. Membership dues were a mark a month, but only 10 per cent of this was forwarded to headquarters. There was the income from Party newspapers, and other publications, and the admission charges and collections at major rallies. Heavy demands were made on members, and the unemployed who formed the core of the S.A. were obliged to hand over their unemployment benefit in return for food and shelter provided in their barracks.

Subsidies came from interested supporters, but information about these is incomplete. Otto Dietrich, a Party member, had family connections with Ruhr industry, and through him Hitler met Emil Kirdorf, who enjoyed himself immensely as guest of honour at the Nuremberg Party Day in 1929. Kirdorf was chief shareholder in the Gelsenkirchen Mine Company, the founder of the Ruhr Coal Syndicate, and controller of the political funds of the Mining Union and North West Association. Another Nazi contact man with the industrial world was Walther Funk, for-merly editor of a leading financial newspaper. In evidence after the war he gave a random list of subscribers from the steel industry, coal mining, banking, the potash industry, and shipping. Fritz Thyssen in his memoirs *I paid Hitler* gives similar information, but what these various intrigues amounted to in terms of cash is uncertain. Funk swore that industry never subscribed more than a total of two million marks to the Nazis before they came to power, and Thyssen mentions two million marks a year, without making it clear what period he is referring to. It may well be true that industrialists subscribed more heavily to Hugenberg's National Party, and that the money raised by the Nazi Party itself has been underestimated.

The number of dues-paying members certainly increased steadily to 49,000 in 1926, 72,000 in 1927, 108,000 in 1928, 178,000 in 1929, 210,000 in March 1930, and nearly 400,000 by the end of the year. A similar sudden rise occurred in popular support. In 1928, 12 Nazi deputies were returned to the Reichstag, and in September 1930, 107, reflecting a vote of over six millions.

Personal feuds, and disagreement over policy, were the inevitable upshot in a movement with no immediate prospect of power. Over two issues Hitler's authority was challenged during the nineteen-twenties. Roehm disagreed with his leader over the role of the S.A., but his departure to South America for some years shelved the matter. A more formidable challenge came from Gregor Strasser, a former army officer and holder of the Iron Cross, who became a Nazi in 1920 and ran a chemist's shop for his living. A massive man, and an able speaker with a strong personality, he emphasized the socialism of the Party programme, and was disinclined to submit to Hitler's authoritarian leadership.

He took part, during Hitler's imprisonment, in election campaigns, in co-operation with other nationalist, anti-semitic parties, which incurred the Fuehrer's wrath, although such activity was the logical concomitant to a policy of legality. Hitler ultimately mollified Strasser and persuaded him to organize the movement in North Germany, where it was practically non-existent.

With the help of Otto, his brother, and Joseph Goebbels, whom he employed as his secretary, Strasser built up a radical movement with its own press, which scarcely recognized Hitler's authority. He preached nationalization and a decentralized system of government, neither of which attracted Hitler. Indeed, Strasser's economic views jeopardized financial support from industry.

The clash between the two wings of the movement crystallized, in 1925, over the question, which excited all Germany, whether the former German royal houses should be deprived of their property or not. Hitler was currently receiving three-quarters of his income from the Duchess of Sachsen-Anhalt, while Strasser spoke out for expropriation, and his line was adopted by a meeting of northern Party leaders at Hanover in November. In the following February, Hitler summoned a party conference at Bamberg in southern Germany. By this time the southern *gauleiters* were full time, salaried Party workers, Hitler's hired hands, and they arrived in strength to support him. Only Strasser and Goebbels could attend a midweek conference from the North, and they were heavily outvoted. Some sort of a truce was concocted, and in the future Strasser seemed incapable of sustained resistance to Hitler, and so the *fuehrerprinzip* was preserved.

The years in the wilderness drew to a close in 1929. The first sign came with the publication of the Young plan for reducing reparation payments. Stresemann accepted the proposals in return for French agreement to a speedier withdrawal from the Rhineland. Hugenberg, leader of the National Party, launched a bitter campaign in Germany against acceptance of the Plan, and enlisted Nazi support. The campaign failed, but Hitler had broken into national politics and attracted the attention of those who controlled the political funds of big business, and the Brown House was furnished on the proceeds. More important was the collapse of the Wall Street Stock Exchange. By 1930 Germany faced economic disaster. The weakness of the Weimar Constitution was again revealed, and the disillusionment and manifold grievances of the German people came to the surface. In September the Nazis won their first major electoral success. Their hour was at hand.

CHAPTER FOUR

The Collapse of German Democracy

SHORTLY after noon on the 30th January 1933, a roar of acclaim rose from the crowds who had gathered all morning outside the Berlin Chancellery. It greeted Adolf Hitler as he appeared on the steps, having been sworn in by the President as Chancellor of Germany. That night thousands of jack-booted stormtroopers tramped through the streets, singing their marching songs and bearing lighted torches aloft so that to the French ambassador they appeared as a 'river of flame'. Nazism had come to power.

Despite the claims of its propagandists, it had not been swept to power on a wave of popular enthusiasm. The Fuehrer had intrigued his way to the Chancellor's office with the connivance of the 'old gang' whom he despised, and the acquiescence of the German people of whom no more than one-third had given positive support to the Nazi Party at the latest Reichstag elections.

The roots of this situation lay to some extent in Germany's distant past, but mainly in more recent events. Unlike Britain, Germany had not enjoyed long centuries of political unity during which liberal democracy could slowly but surely take root. The Weimar Constitution, its first democratic experiment, proved so defective as to be unworkable. Political parties and other powerful interests failed to resolve their particular conflicting aims in order to make democracy a living force, their only bond being a common hatred for the Versailles settlement of 1919 which created a mood of rabid nationalism. The mass of the people were bewildered by the march of events, contemptuous of politicians who substituted intrigues for policies, and embittered by social and economic hardship.

In 1648 the Peace of Westphalia had completed the disintegration of medieval Germany into more than 300 independent states. During the eighteenth century there had begun the Austro-Prussian struggle for German supremacy which was resolved by Bismarck in 1871, when he united Germany under Prussian leadership to the exclusion of Austria and her own ramshackle empire in south-eastern Europe. The Second Reich, which he had wrought by 'blood and iron', was given a superficially democratic constitution but was in practice an autocracy. The Hohenzollern emperors and their advisers ruled Germany until the Revolution of 1918. In the following year the Weimar Constitution was applied to a people without experience of or mature feeling for the spirit of tolerance and honourable compromise which is essential to the working of parliamentary democracy.

The constitution of 1919 was a democratic instrument of government which theoretically prevented abuse of power by any of its component parts. Universal suffrage was established, and a Reichstag elected on a basis of proportional representation. The President held office by popular election, appointed and dismissed the Chancellor and his cabinet, and could dissolve the Reichstag. The principle of ministerial responsibility to the Reichstag was established, and provision made for plebiscites to be held in certain circumstances. A federal structure was retained, although the powers of individual states were fewer than those of the semi-autonomous kingdoms within the Empire. All this was based on intellectual appreciations of the working of parliamentary democracy in other parts of the world. It was not, as it could not be, born out of the accumulated experience of the German people.

In practice the system of proportional representation, whereby each party fighting an election sent one member to the Reichstag for every 60,000 votes it polled, led to every shade of interest being represented but no single party ever commanding a majority. In 1930, for example, ten parties polled over one million votes each. Coalitions were necessary in order to carry on parliamentary government at all, but it was administrative necessity alone which produced them.

Coalition government need not have meant weak government. In the Prussian state parliament, Social Democrats and Centre Party enjoyed a steady majority which made Prussia the bulwark of German democracy. But in the Reichstag the coalition of Social Democrats, Centre and Democrats, which had been responsible for the constitution, never again won a majority after 1919. They could only form a ministry which commanded a Reichstag majority by taking in other parties, who were won over temporarily by deals which rendered firmness of policy unlikely. Neither of the major opposition parties, the National Party and the Communists, were themselves able to construct an alternative coalition.

Party leaders became absorbed in political horse-trading to such an extent that weak government suited them quite well, in that it left those in power more subject to party pressure. There was little sense of loyalty among party members to their cabinet representatives, and no minister was free from the danger of betrayal by his own followers.

Perhaps only the ability and integrity of an a-political civil service prevented the machinery of government grinding to a halt. But while the politicians manoeuvred for power the civil service found its role frustrated. During Hitler's trial in 1924, the State Secretary of the Minister of the Interior informed the court that his office had accumulated considerable evidence of the treasonable activities of the Nazi Party, but no action had been taken. Further recommendations were made by the police authorities in 1930 for the dismantling of the Nazi movement, again with no result.

Aggravated by the economic crisis beginning in 1929, the difficulties of parliamentary government were such that some modification of the existing pattern was probably unavoidable. Those who framed the constitution, apparently not trusting in the capacity of democratic society to overcome its crises, had provided a temporary remedy in Article 48, which enabled legislation to be put into effect by Presidential decree. In July 1930, Heinrich Bruening's administration, which had painfully assembled a new coalition for each item of legislation, found part of its fiscal programme rejected in the Reichstag. With President Hindenburg's agreement, Bruening resorted to Article 48, and in practice parliamentary government had come to an end. Whether Bruening himself, or those who opposed him, bore the greater responsibility for this is still a matter of dispute.

Certainly every important political party in Germany had contributed in some measure to this situation, and was also to share responsibility for it being resolved as it was in January 1933.

Least culpable, perhaps, were the Social Democrats, for they at least remained loyal to the Republic which they had founded; but they lacked a coherent policy and strong leadership. Well before 1918 the welfare services established under the Hohenzollerns had drawn the sting from militant socialism. Like many English Labour leaders after 1918, the majority of Social Democrats were eager to gain acceptance as moderate, responsible, and above all, respectable men. From the beginning they were saddled with the odium of having surrendered to the allies in 1918, and accepting the dictated peace of 1919. In neither circumstance did they have any alternative, as the military High Command admitted in private. But they were made the scapegoats, as much by the army as anyone else, for these disasters. Furthermore, Fritz Ebert's provisional government had suppressed the German Revolution of 1918–19 only with the help of the army. The Soldiers' and Workers' Councils were foiled, and the Spartakists destroyed, but in return Ebert allowed the Officer Corps to retain much of its pre-war prestige, enabling it to become again one of the most powerful factors in German politics.

The potential strength of the party was dramatically illustrated by its response to the Kapp *Putsch*, an extreme right wing attempt to overthrow the Republic in 1920, led by Wolfgang Kapp and General von Luttwitz, supported by several of the *Freikorps*. The army remained uncommitted, and a general strike, proclaimed by the government and loyally supported by the trade unions, was instrumental in restoring the constitution. But as the nineteen-twenties wore on, the Social Democrats appeared less as a dynamic force and increasingly as a conservative trade-union party. They opposed Nazism and appreciated its nature. But lacking leadership, they faltered sadly in 1932, when Papen's government suppressed democratic government in Prussia. Karl Severing made no more than a nominal gesture of defiance, when a general strike might have worked as it had in 1920. Ultimately, in 1933, they made a courageous last stand. By then it was too late, but at least they had kept their dignity and self-respect, which is more than may be said of any other party.

Notoriously ready to reach an accommodation with any government in order to preserve its particular interests, the Catholic Centre Party was as much concerned to preserve Catholic schools as effective parliamentary government. In 1932 it showed some independence in refusing to support Franz von Papen, one of its number, when he cynically replaced Bruening, a fellow member, in the position of Chancellor, but it was ready to compromise with Nazism, and was blindly to continue negotiation to this end until there remained nothing to be negotiated. The Reichstag votes of the Centre Party were cast even for the Enabling Law, which conferred overriding power on Hitler after he had become Chancellor.

The lack of a strong liberal party in Weimar Germany was one of its many disasters. But the fortunes of liberalism were waning throughout Europe between the two world wars, and it is perhaps worth emphasizing that Germany was but one of a number of countries where liberty vanished under some form of dictatorship. The People's Party and the Democrats, who might have fulfilled the liberal role in Germany, suffered a more severe loss of votes to the Nazis than any other party, which alone demonstrates how inadequate they were as a source of opposition to totalitarianism.

Although it fought elections and sent members to the Reichstag, the German Communist Party (K.P.D.) was inevitably unreconciled to parliamentary government, and made four abortive bids for power between 1918 and 1923. Its fortunes slumped during the prosperous years between 1924 and 1929, but with the Depression it revived to win six million votes in 1932. Long before then it had become the docile instrument of Comintern. Its policies reflected Russian requirements and bore little relation to the realities of German politics. The lack of political judgment of Ernst Thaelmann and its other leaders is almost beyond belief.

In following the dictates of Stalin, the K.P.D. came to believe that from a working-class point of view there was nothing to choose between bourgeois democracy and Nazi dictatorship. The Social Democrats were held to have betrayed the workers by their adherence to such a democracy. When the Weimar régime was replaced by Nazism, the fraudulent and misleading attraction of social democracy would disappear, and inevitably the workers would unite behind the K.P.D. to establish the dictatorship of the proletariat. The Red Front's street brawls with the S.A. were therefore of little political significance; the fact that the Nazis were the most important mass party in Germany after 1930 was one the blinkered marxists refused to recognize.

The very existence of a strong Communist Party lent weight to Nazi propaganda when it claimed to be Germany's protection against Bolshevism, and many Germans, perceiving only a choice between two evils, voted for Nazism as the lesser of them. Furthermore, in creating public disorder, attacking the Social Democrats, and undermining in any way open to them the whole Weimar structure, the K.P.D. was simply helping Nazism along the road to power. Later claims that communism led the struggle against the National-Socialists are not borne out by existing evidence.

The influence of Communism is not to be exaggerated, and the most guilty of all Germany's political parties was the National Party. Claiming to be a Conservative party, it forsook its true role in favour of reaction, and was deeply involved in enabling the consummation of the Nazi revolution.

It never reconciled itself to the loss of the war and the disappearance of the monarchy. Wealthy, and with the support of powerful landed and industrial interests, it refused, except for two brief periods, to share the responsibility of government, preferring irresponsible and disloyal opposition, in the belief, which it shared with the K.P.D., that when the Weimar republic collapsed, power would pass into its hands. Its leader, Alfred Hugenberg, the newspaper and film magnate, was the worst type of political boss, and it was associated with the strongly nationalist ex-servicemen's association, the *Stalhelm*. The political activities of the Nationalists included incitement to murder and sending parcels of human excrement through the post to their opponents. By 1930 they were clearly ready to do a deal with Hitler. Already Hugenberg had financed the Nazis in order to win their active support in his campaign against the Young Plan for modifying reparations.

With the collapse of normal parliamentary government, considerable responsibility devolved upon the President. With no Reichstag majority to guide him, the only available criteria in selecting Chancellor and ministers were his own judgment of their merits, and his assessment of their chance of securing adequate support. Pending such support he was obliged to decide how frequently, and for what purposes, he would use his emergency powers.

It had been hoped in 1919 that a popularly elected President would act as a check on the Reichstag. French history was taken to show that Presidents elected by Parliament were almost invariably mediocrities, while American experience demonstrated the merit of a popular President. But a mediocrity with political experience is better than a popular figure with none. The latter contingency is avoided in the U.S.A. by the existence of a mature two-party system, but Germany had no such safeguard, and in 1925 Field-Marshal von Hindenburg was elected. Hindenburg was not the man to deal with political crises. On the night of 9th November 1918, while General Groener had undertaken the monumental responsibility of reaching an accommodation on behalf of the Army with the newly established republican government in Berlin, Hindenburg had lain a few yards away, asleep,

emotionally prostrate, leaving his nominal subordinate to negotiate over the telephone for the future of the Army and possibly
even the Reich itself.

For nearly five years his political ineptitude had no ill effect.
Indeed the fact that he was head of the state and Supreme Commander of the Army did much to reconcile conservative Germans
to the Republic, and his respect for the constitution disarmed
those who attacked the Republic as a betrayal of national interests. But these were years of prosperity. When economic
depression precipitated political crisis after 1930, Hindenburg's
true quality was revealed. He grew senile, tending to believe what
was said to him by the last person to whom he spoke, and his
inability to judge the respective merits of those who jockeyed
for power around him was fatal.

While the Berlin government floundered, the federal structure
of Germany aggravated rather than eased its difficulties. In 1919,
Hugo Preuss had advocated a centralized unitary state. Instead,
seventeen *Lands*, ranging from Prussia with a population of
nearly 40 million to Schaumburg-Lippe with only 48,000, retained
certain independent powers, including control of police. Each
had a *Landtag*, which tended to be a microcosm of the Reichstag with all its defects.

Local particularism was strong in Bavaria where, ever since
the unification of Germany, there had been marked dislike of
government from Berlin, and after 1918 there was sympathy for
secession and a South German Union with Austria. In 1920 a
strong right-wing government seized power, and Bavaria became
the Mecca for all who opposed the Republic. Here the remnants
of the *Freikorps* gathered, and a variety of nationalist organizations sprouted. It was no accident that the National-Socialist
party was born in Munich and that a Bavarian Minister of Justice,
Franz Guertner, was one of its earliest protectors in high places.

The small size of several *Lands* made it possible for a determined party to concentrate all its resources to win power, con-
stitutionally, in one. This the Nazis did in Brunswick, thus gaining
useful administrative experience and a base from which to pro-

mote their activities. It was the Brunswick State Government which made Hitler a German national, without questions asked, when he decided to run for the Reich Presidency in 1932.

As in any democracy, there existed in Weimar Germany powerful vested interests whose functions were not primarily political, but who acted as pressure groups to persuade the politicians to meet their special requirements. On the whole these interested groups were hostile to the Republic. The Trade Unions alone were committed to support it, but on the whole they suffered the same defects as the Social Democrats. Economic depressions weakened their membership, and although they resisted Communist infiltration after 1930 they failed to perceive the threat of Nazism. Until faced by a *fait accompli* their leaders assumed that not even the Nazis would risk an open attack on such a well-established institution.

Industry and big business were from the outset hostile to the Republic and democracy. Fritz Thyssen of United Steel, I. G. Farben the great dye trust, Krupp the armaments firm and others were prepared to finance parties hostile to it. At first the National Party enjoyed most of their munificence, but in time more of it was diverted into the funds of the Nazis.

Nor were the landowners any more amenable to the new order after the war. Despite the assistance given to East Prussian landowners, which became a financial scandal, the Junkers remained unreconciled and their Land League, led by Graf Kalkreuth, was always one element in the opposition to democracy. Like the National Party, which they generally supported, these elements of German society pursued the immoral course of seeking power while avoiding responsibility.

Most powerful of these vested interests was the *Reichswehr*, the German Army, which in the final analysis was the only body which alone might have saved Germany from Nazism, even at the eleventh hour. The Officer Corps, steeped in autocratic Prussian tradition, had enjoyed a position of immense privilege and prestige in Imperial Germany. It elected its own members, who were not answerable for their conduct to any civilian court but only their own Courts of Honour. Theoretically, its power was diminished under the Republic, but in practice it was still largely its own master. That the Republic had survived its early difficulties at all was in part due to the Army, which in return won wide freedom from civil interference in its affairs.

Having insisted that an armistice was inevitable, and rejection of the allied peace terms impossible, the German Army returned home in good order — a triumph of logistics and a tribute to the professional ability of its officers — and proceeded to rationalize its defeat. That it was the victim of a 'stab in the back' inflicted by civilian authorities was a convenient explanation. Indeed it was no soldier, but President Ebert who greeted the returning army with the words: 'I salute you, who have returned unvanquished from the field of battle.'

Humiliated by the limitations imposed upon it at Versailles, in numbers of men and quantities of equipment, the *Reichswehr* settled down to prepare for the day of reckoning. Hans von Seeckt, its second post-war commander, did much, with the connivance of the government, to evade the restrictions imposed by the allies. Selective recruitment created an army of potential officers and N.C.O.s; state police forces and para-military organizations like the S.A. were given sidearms and treated as reservoirs of manpower. Agreements with Soviet Russia allowed clandestine rearmament to take place there.

Politically the Army had no sympathy for the Republic. Seeckt saw the *Reichswehr* as a state within a state, and laid down the principle that it must be above politics so that it could fulfil its primary role as guardian of the state. It was to the Reich and not to the Republic that its loyalty lay, as was evidenced by its equivocal attitude during the Kapp *Putsch*. While the maintenance of the Republic was clearly necessary to the preservation of the Reich, the Army would uphold it, but if necessary it would be discarded without regret.

Seeckt's policy was illustrated in 1923. Faced with the dangerous Bavarian situation, the Reich cabinet could find no other solution than to transfer executive power into the hands of the

Minister of Defence, which in practice meant those of Seeckt. The Bavarian dissidents were brought to heel, and the Army was clearly the arbiter of national politics and the guarantor of German unity. But Seeckt had not acted to preserve democracy. Had he believed that the Nationalist movement offered a genuine remedy for Germany's ills, he would not have hesitated to swing the power of the *Reichswehr* behind it.

Under Seeckt, a man of integrity and perception, the Army would not necessarily have preserved the Weimar Constitution indefinitely, but it might well have saved Germany and Europe from Nazism. Unfortunately Seeckt's power declined after Hindenburg's election as President in 1925, and an indiscretion in 1926 was only the occasion of his resignation. For a time the person of Hindenburg bound the Army and Republic more closely together, but Hindenburg was to prove a broken reed.

Increasingly, real power in the Army was drawn into the hands of Kurt von Schleicher. A successful staff-officer, he became, in 1928, right-hand man to General Groener when the latter was appointed Minister of Defence. He was a born manipulator and intriguer, and sought constitutional reform to provide stable government. To this end he hoped to construct a right wing coalition into which he could draw the Nazis, whose mass support he valued. The intrigues to which he was thus committed played no small part in Hitler's rise to power.

With fatal results, Schleicher had dragged the Army down into the political arena and committed it to one side. He first abandoned Seeckt's principle when he used his influence to secure the appointment of Bruening as Chancellor in 1930. By 1932 the effect of this involvement in politics was transparently clear when Schleicher avowed that the Army was unable — in fact it was unwilling — to fire on the S.A. should civil war break out.

By the early nineteen-thirties, nearly all the powerful interests in Germany were prepared to jettison the existing system in return for one which would gratify their particular ends. To achieve this purpose most of them were prepared to use Nazism. This was not because they were themselves nazi in outlook; they were not rabid anti-semites, they disapproved in many cases of the strong-arm methods of the S.A., and they distrusted the radical wing of the movement led by Strasser. However, they were prepared to overlook these things in the mistaken belief that when given a share of power the Nazis would prove more tractable. They had a certain community of interest with National-Socialism in that they did not feel necessarily committed to preserve the constitution, and in their dislike of the Versailles Treaty, but what really turned them to Nazism was the mass support it had begun to attract.

While their elected representatives gave no clear lead, the German people grew disillusioned with the democratic experiment and its failure, in particular, to solve their pressing material problems, and popular support for the National-Socialist Party grew.

During the war Germany suffered excessive exploitation of her economic resources, a reduction in population, and a decline in standards of health. The Versailles settlement had reduced her cultivable land and her mineral resources, while reparations imposed heavy burdens for the future. Germany had become a debtor rather than a creditor nation.

An unsatisfactory policy during the war, based on loans rather than taxation, created inflationary tendencies which were not checked after the war ended, and during 1922 the mark declined sharply in value. In 1923 it collapsed, and the exchange rate reached 4200 billion marks to the dollar.

As a result small and medium sized estates, in the form of bank deposits, securities and mortgages, were liquidated. In future the middle class, its savings gone, was obliged to rely on income from labour, and small and medium incomes were not quickly re-established. Big business was enabled, by the destruction of the currency, to wipe out its debts by the payment of worthless marks, and many great industrialists and landlords emerged economically stronger from the crisis. Thus was created a gulf between the rich and the unpropertied masses. How this had come about was little understood, but the human contrast between rich and poor was evident and the government deservedly blamed.

The inflationary spiral could have been checked by balancing the budget and, although difficult, this was not impossible had adequate taxation been imposed on those able to pay. As it was, inflation was allowed to run its course, partly to evade reparation payments, and to embarrass the French who had reoccupied the Ruhr in order to exact them, with disastrous social consequences.

The situation also allowed into German economic life an influx of foreigners, since a small capital in dollar currency was worth a great deal of money. Hence there was an intensification of the hatred of capitalism (which passed for socialism) and nationalism based on hostility to foreigners.

The economic revival between 1924 and 1930 was one of superficial prosperity based on short term loans at high rates of interest. It did not, in any case, erase the memory of lost savings or the fear of unemployment, and by 1931 these nightmares were again a vivid reality for thousands of Germans.

The collapse of the Wall Street Stock Exchange in New York, in 1929, soon repercussed in Germany as a banking crisis and led to a severe industrial slump. Short term loans were called in by foreign creditors, while a rapid contraction of world trade made it increasingly difficult for Germany — as for other nations beset by similar problems — to pay her way by increasing exports.

The most significant social consequence of the slump was the steep rise in unemployment from 1,320,000 in September 1929 to some 6,000,000 in early 1932. In human terms these statistics were school leavers without hope of a job, men standing aimlessly on street corners and women made distraught by the lack of food and heating in their families' homes. The middle class, largely shorn of its savings in 1923, found the prospect of losing its livelihood even more frightening than did working men. For them it entailed the social disgrace of descent to the status of artisans and labourers, and in their anxiety many turned to the Nazi movement, led as it was by a man who had shared their social snobbery in pre-war Vienna.

More than any other single factor the Depression gave the

Nazis their opportunity. In 1928 they held 12 seats in the Reichstag; in 1930 they won 107 and in July 1932, 230. Thereafter their popular support was in decline, but it remained considerable and they were established as a major political party. Hence the readiness of those in power to reach an accommodation with them.

In their search for a scapegoat to answer for their disasters the Germans found several, each of which chimed conveniently with what the Nazis had been saying for a decade. First there was the corruption and inadequacy of parliamentary government which must have seemed all too apparent. There was also the hated *Diktat* of Versailles, which created universal resentment in Germany. The European territory lost included much that had been acquired by naked force, but also areas where there was a high proportion of German-speaking people. President Wilson's principle of national self-determination, it could be argued, had been applied only where the allies saw fit. The Polish corridor cut the Reich in two to meet the needs of one of Germany's traditional enemies. Germany's overseas colonies had been mandated to various of the allies, but this too could be interpreted as naked Franco-British imperialism. The army was reduced to 10,000 men, shorn of its General Staff and deprived of aircraft and tanks. Reparations were demanded in gold marks, coal, ships, timber, cattle and other items. These burdens may or may not have been payable, but the implication of Germany's 'war guilt' that went with them incensed the whole nation. Neither the Dawes Plan, 1924, nor the Young Plan, 1929, acted as a palliative. Indeed the governments which accepted them incurred further odium for the Republic which had accepted the original demands.

After more than forty years it seems that the allied statesmen would have done well to moderate their demands in 1919, but the temper of the times was against them. Although the Germans claim to have been harshly treated is not without foundation, such evidence as exists suggests that as victors they would have been no more generous. The abortive peace of Brest-Litovsk, imposed on defeated Russia in 1918, deprived her of nearly one-third of her population, one-third of her railway mileage, 73 per cent of her iron ore, 89 per cent of her coal and over 5,000 industrial premises. In addition Russia was to pay an indemnity of six billion marks. In contrast Versailles left the Reich geographically intact, politically united and with most of her potential strength as a great nation.

The hatred for a peace imposed by foreigners engendered a distrust of foreigners in which there grew a vein of anti-semitism. Hatred of the Jews had been an Austrian rather than a German characteristic before 1914. German Jews had been hard-working, intelligent and patriotic. After 1918 an uncontrolled influx of foreign Jews from the East took place. The newcomers were accustomed to a lower standard of living and prepared to accept lower wages. Their habits, dress, frequent ignorance of the German language, and tendency to crowd together in rather shabby colonies earned, not only for them but for all Jews, increased distaste. Some of the foreign speculators who had done well in 1923 were foreign Jews, and some of the more spectacular financial scandals of Weimar Germany involved Jewish businessmen, while much of the publishing and entertainment industries, particularly their seamy sides, appears to have been in Jewish hands.

With the Republic visibly disintegrating the Nazis were ready to grasp their long awaited opportunity. Hitler had believed, as only a monomaniac can, that his day would come. His drive for power, and the skill with which Nazism exploited and focused the incoherent resentments of a distracted and disillusioned people, are factors of prime importance in explaining the replacement of democracy by totalitarianism.

From the beginning Hitler had been unsparing in his attacks on the Republic, the Versailles Treaty, the forces of reaction and the Jews. Shrewdly he appreciated the importance of the Army, and as early as his trial in 1924 he took the opportunity to emphasize that the *Reichswehr* and the Party had a common goal in the creation of a greater Germany. To the industrialists also he spoke soothing words. In January 1932, Fritz Thyssen arranged for him to address the Industry Club at Dusseldorf. Emphatically he told his audience of his 'inexorable decision to destroy Marxism in Germany' with such persuasiveness that the hard-bitten tycoons, who had received him coolly, gave him a standing ovation as he sat down. Nazism's opposition to communism was the strongest element in its appeal to the propertied classes.

With perceptive demagogy Nazi orators fed and directed the resentments of the German people. The Republic was corrupt; the French bent on enslaving them; the speculators prospered at the expense of working men; the Marxists preached class hatred to divide the nation and everywhere the Jews battened on the Fatherland. Existing parties and politicians were tainted with the 'System' and Germany must look to new men to recover her place in the sun.

In this kind of agitation the Nazis were unrivalled. The Communists alone could match them in style, but their rigid doctrines limited their appeal, whereas the Nazis, devoid of any principle or belief, save their inherent right to power, changed their tune to suit their audience. Radicalism was the Communist high card, since Hitler could not allow his own radicals too much scope for fear of alienating the industrialists. But the Nazis held the trumps of anti-semitism and nationalism.

By the autumn of 1931 democratic government in Germany was virtually dead. Power rested with President Hindenburg and the men round him. They knew that to prolong government by emergency decree indefinitely was not possible, and that some permanent rearrangement was imperative. What form it should take was not agreed; it need not necessarily be parliamentary, but it required at least the acquiescence of the German people. Recent elections suggested that Hitler might provide this if he could be brought into the government as a junior partner. The nature of Nazism was not understood and the tactical ability of its Fuehrer greatly underrated. In these circumstances there began the involved sequence of events and intrigue which brought Nazism to power.

CHAPTER FIVE

The Tortuous Path to Power

THE MEN who disposed of power in the twilight of the Weimar Republic were President Hindenburg, and his son and adjutant, Oskar; Otto Meissner, the head of the Presidential Chancery; General von Schleicher, who was head of a bureau in the defence ministry which handled the political and press affairs of the Army and Navy; Heinrich Bruening and, after his fall, Franz von Papen who succeeded him as Chancellor.

These men were looking for a government which would take resolute action to deal with the current political and economic crisis, but at the same time win some mass support, preferably a Reichstag majority. Bruening, it became clear, was not going to accomplish this, and Schleicher thought Hitler worth considering as a partner. Not only had he six million votes, but the S.A. threatened armed revolution if the Nazi claims to power were not met.

Hitler's tactics were to use the threat of rebellion, which he hoped to avoid, and the promise of mass support, which he seemed unable to convert into an outright majority, as the means with which to persuade the presidential group to give him power. At the back of his mind the Fuehrer still considered the possibility of a coalition with the National Party, or even the Centre; or, preferably, of winning an outright majority at the next election. Each time negotiations with the presidential group broke down he returned to these alternatives. But it appears that his main purpose in doing so was to secure the resumption of talks, and the measures he took intended to put pressure on the governing clique to that end.

The first series of negotiations was an abortive attempt to reach some measure of agreement between Bruening and Hitler. Bruening had few illusions about Nazism, and it was Schleicher, who was convinced that it could be used and controlled, who made the first moves.

Schleicher met Hitler unofficially, through Ernst Roehm, in the autumn of 1931, and used his considerable powers of persuasion to arrange for Hitler to meet both Bruening and Hindenburg.

Bruening asked for Hitler's support until he had settled the reparations question, and secured the re-election of Hindenburg as President. Whereupon, he promised, he would resign to allow someone more acceptable to the parties of the right to replace him. Hitler's replies were vague, and the talks ended inconclusively. Precisely what happened when the Fuehrer met Hindenburg, shortly afterwards, is not known, but it seems likely that Hitler talked too much and the President was not impressed, remarking afterwards that Hitler might make a Minister of Posts, but not a Chancellor.

Immediately Hitler shifted his ground to participate in the so-called 'Harzburg Front' on 11th October 1931. The occasion was a meeting of right wing interests. Among those present were Hugenberg, Seldte and Deusterberg, the leaders of the *Stalhelm*, Dr. Schacht, Hans von Seeckt, Graf Kalkreuth, and representatives of the Ruhr and Rhineland industries. A solemn resolution was passed uniting all parties of the right, and demanding that Bruening, and Braun, the Prime Minister of Prussia, should resign to allow Reich and Prussian elections to take place.

Hitler's presence was no more than a tactical manoeuvre. He was not at ease in the Harzburg gathering, which was made up of the 'old gang' whom he so frequently criticized. Too close an association with them would lose him mass support. Indeed, Hitler left the meeting before its end, piqued, no doubt, because the *Stalhelm* detachments present heavily outnumbered the S.A.

Further to emphasize his anger at being rejected by those in power, Hitler launched a series of scathing attacks on Bruening, as the embodiment of the 'System' under which Germany had been governed since 1918. Added weight was given to these criticisms by the provincial elections in Hesse, in November 1931, when the Nazis won a resounding success, indicating that there had been a marked increase in their popular support since the Reichstag elections of September 1930, which had made them a significant party for the first time.

Nazism's continued electoral success only confirmed Schleicher in his views, and he continued talks with Hitler during the winter, even, according to one authority, convincing General Groener, his chief at the Defence Ministry, of the wisdom of his policy.

Bruening remained more realistic, but at the same time he needed Nazi support. He was concerned to secure Hindenburg's re-election as President, believing that only Hindenburg would continue to sign the decrees placed before him, thus enabling the Chancellor to continue in office until economic conditions improved, or some success had been won in the field of foreign policy.

Hindenburg was not eager to remain in office; he was an old man with no illusions about the strain an election campaign would impose on him. He agreed, however, to remain, if Bruening could secure prolongation of his office by the permissible means of obtaining the agreement of two-thirds of the Reichstag. Bruening was prepared to attempt this: the man who had relinquished the search for a parliamentary majority in favour of government by decree, was ready to seek one more majority in order to continue ruling by decree. To achieve his *ad hoc* coalition he needed the Nazis. Why he should have supposed that they might help him to strengthen his own position, even temporarily, is not clear.

Simultaneous offers were made both to Hitler and Hugenberg in January 1932. Broadly they were those made to Hitler in the previous October, although it is possible that Bruening promised to support Hitler for the Chancellorship. Hugenberg quickly rejected the offers, and Hitler eventually did the same, after some dispute within the Party which may or may not have influenced his decision.

In his reply to the government the Fuehrer made a direct offer to Hindenburg, to support the prolongation of his presidency if he would dismiss Bruening and hold elections to the Reichstag and Prussian diet. This offer Hindenburg dismissed out of hand, whereupon Hitler launched another furious attack on Bruening in two open letters. Twice he had glimpsed power only to have it snatched from him, largely as a result of his unswerving determination to have it on his own terms.

The next stage in events was dictated by Bruening's situation. To retain power he needed Hindenburg and so had no alternative but to get him returned at the forthcoming election. In this he had the temporary support of Schleicher, who also felt it imperative to keep the old field-marshal where he was, while his own schemes matured. Hindenburg himself had been angered by the refusal of the right to support prolongation of his term of office, and agreed to stand.

After some hesitation, acutely reflected in Goebbel's diary for the period, Hitler decided to stand as a candidate himself. The National Party ran Duesterberg, the second in command of the *Stalhelm*, and the Communists, Ernst Thaelmann.

With the election arranged for 13th March 1932, every party launched itself on a campaign of remarkable bitterness. Bruening, with no doubts about what was at stake, ruthlessly reserved all radio time on government controlled networks for his own side. The Communists, following the line dictated from Moscow, concentrated their attacks on the Social Democrats and trade unions.

But all efforts paled before the Nazi campaign. Following Hitler's speech to the Industry Club in Dusseldorf, in January, there was no shortage of money. Every constituency was thoroughly canvassed. The walls of towns were plastered with highly coloured posters. Films were made of Hitler and Goebbels, and shown all over Germany. Gramophone records were made which could be sent through the post, and played over loudspeakers mounted on

C

lorries. Eight million pamphlets, and twelve million extra copies of party newspapers, were distributed. As many as three thousand meetings were held in one day, and as much as two hundred thousand marks spent on propaganda in one week. True to Hitler's belief in the spoken word, he and his lieutenants addressed huge crowds throughout Germany in the most unbridled terms. Goebbel's programme has been reconstructed from his diary. Between 22nd February and 12th March, he made nineteen speeches in Berlin and addressed mass meetings in nine other major towns scattered across Germany.

In contrast Hindenburg spoke only once, in a recorded broadcast. His restraint must have won him many thousands of votes, when he said: 'I ask for no votes from those who do not wish to vote for me.'

The party alignments in March 1932 gave a clear illustration of the confused state of German politics. Hindenburg, a Prussian, belonging by rights to the National Party, a Protestant, and a monarchist at heart, won most of his support from the Social Democrats, the trade unions, the Catholic Centre and other small democratic parties; for all of these he had become the personification of the Weimar Constitution. The Conservative upper classes of the Protestant north voted either for Duesterberg or for Hitler, while some working-class votes were attracted to the Communist candidate.

Tension was not eased when the results of a very heavy poll were announced. The Nazi popular vote was seen to have increased since the previous autumn by 86 per cent, but was some 7 millions behind Hindenburg. The latter, however, had just failed, by under 200,000 votes, to win an outright majority over his three opponents, and a second election was necessary.

For the second campaign the ingenious Goebbels hit on the novel stunt of the Fuehrer covering Germany by aeroplane. This he did, on one occasion flying to an engagement in Dusseldorf when violent storms had supposedly grounded all air traffic over Western Germany. Eagerly, the Nazi press dramatized this as a clear indication of Hitler's quality as a leader. In fact the Fuehrer's

PLATE II. This Nazi rally in the late nineteen-thirties contrasts
strongly with the early street-corner methods of propaganda.

foolhardiness was in vain. Again he increased his popular vote to well over 13 millions, but Hindenburg was comfortably home with 53 per cent of the poll.

Immediately after the presidential elections, state elections were due, in April, in Prussia and elsewhere. Prussia was vital on account of its size. The Nazi propaganda machine again went into action, with Hitler making a second series of well-publicized flights. In Prussia the Nazis became the largest single party but were unable to form a majority coalition, even with the Nationalists. Comparable gains were made in the other provincial elections, but with similar result. Nazism's popular appeal had been remarkable but insufficient. In addition the government felt strong enough to take action against it, and dissension broke out in the ranks of the movement itself.

As early as November 1931, evidence had come to light in Hesse, that the S.A. had detailed plans for defeating a Communist rising — should it occur — and establishing a provisional Nazi government. These revelations created a sensation and embarrassed Hitler, who knew nothing of them. Typically the Reich government refused to act, but increasing evidence of schemes for an S.A. *Putsch* were uncovered at the time of the presidential elections, and the State Governments presented Groener, the Minister of the Interior, with an ultimatum, that if he did not act they would do so independently. Faced with this, Groener overcame Bruening's incomprehensible opposition, and on 14th April 1932, a Reich decree dissolved the S.A. and the S.S. Hitler overcame Roehm's instinctive impulse to resist, and the Brownshirts vanished. Not that they were disbanded; their organization remained intact while they masqueraded as ordinary party members.

Frustrated by the elections the party dissidents began to express their displeasure. Roehm, before his organization was driven undercover, was already prepared to risk armed rebellion. At local level his men grew increasingly restless. On a more sophisticated plane, Gregor Strasser returned to the arguments he had adopted before the elections; that Hitler should be prepared to

compromise with those in power, and that his 'policy of legality'
was being wrecked by his refusal to do so. For the moment Hitler
had no answer save his own intuitive political judgment, which
was not to play him false.

It is possible that at this juncture the government could still
have saved Germany from the Nazis, but a third phase in the
struggle for power was begun by the *eminence grise* of German
politics in 1932, Kurt von Schleicher.

The 'intriguer', as his name aptly means, had continued
throughout most of the spring to keep in touch with the Nazi
movement through Roehm, with whom he discussed a variety of
schemes. None of them was helped by the ban on the S.A., which
he opposed, and he set out to undermine the man responsible.
He persuaded Hindenburg to write to Groener implying that the
ban was unfair, in that the *Reichsbanner*, the Social Democrat
organization (which was in fact unarmed), had not been touched.
A malicious whispering campaign was begun against the Defence
Minister, aided by vituperative attacks from Nazi deputies in
the Reichstag. Schleicher himself administered the *coup de grâce*
by informing his chief that the Army no longer had confidence
in him. Despite Bruening's loyal support, Groener was obliged to
resign, and his going was a further blow to the Republic. It was
he who had negotiated for the Army with the government in
1918. He had promised the Army's support to the new régime
and he personally had kept his word. There was no other general
to replace him.

Schleicher now saw Bruening as a further obstacle to reaching
agreement with the Nazis, and determined to unseat him.
Already Bruening's position was weak. The Depression was still
severe, the postponement of the Lausanne Conference prevented
settlement of the reparations issue, and French opposition at
Geneva had so far frustrated his attempts to secure equality in
armaments for Germany. The industrialists disliked attempts to
restrict prices, and his plans to use bankrupt estates in East
Germany for land colonization were denounced by the Junkers as
'Agrarian Bolshevism'. Ironically, his success in securing Hinden-

burg's re-election weakened him. The President began to resent him, as the man who had forced him into an election campaign, and felt nothing but sympathy for the Junkers of whom he was one. Schleicher played on these feelings with a persuasive tongue, and eventually used his insurmountable argument that the Chancellor no longer enjoyed the confidence of the Army. On 30th May Bruening resigned at Hindenburg's request. The Nazi leaders had done little to bring about his fall, although they were kept informed of what was happening. The responsibility for it was almost entirely Schleicher's.

Waiting in the wings for his cue was Schleicher's next protégé for the Chancellor's office, Franz von Papen, whose period of power demarcates the next stage of events.

Papen was a member of the Westphalian aristocracy, a former cavalry officer and gentleman rider. His manner was impeccable and his political morality non-existent. Nominally he was a member of the Catholic Centre, but sat in the Prussian diet in opposition to his party's coalition with the Social Democrats. He had never sat in the Reichstag, and personified the reactionary character of post-war German conservatism. Schleicher recommended him to the President in the mistaken belief that he could be easily manipulated; Hindenburg accepted him, easily won over by his superficial charm.

Publicly, the appointment caused an outcry, which Papen's ministers did nothing to pacify. The 'Cabinet of Barons' contained no outstanding political figure. Seven belonged to the aristocracy, two had connections with big business, and the tenth was Franz Guertner, Hitler's one-time protector in Bavaria. It had no hope of Reichstag support. The Centre was indignant at Bruening's dismissal, Hugenberg was annoyed because he had not been invited to replace Bruening, and Social Democrats and Communists inevitably opposed such a ministry.

Thus the Nazis were Papen's only hope of mass support, and this provides the key to the political background of Papen's chancellorship. Papen and Schleicher believed that Hitler would be prepared to compromise with them if his party failed to achieve power by an outright majority. The basic questions between May 1932 and January 1933 were whether or not a bargain could be struck, and, if so, on whose terms. Papen and Schleicher believed they could win Nazi support for less than Hitler demanded, and, when he rejected their offers, they ignored him, hoping that the strain on the party would force his hand. In contrast Hitler was determined not to yield. Further complications were added to this pattern by the growing animosity between Papen and Schleicher, and disagreement over tactics between Hitler and Strasser.

Papen bought temporary Nazi acquiescence in his government by dissolving the Reichstag, which in any case he dared not face, and lifting the ban on the S.A. This was accurately described by Thaelmann as open provocation to murder, and in the next few weeks scores of people were killed and hundreds wounded in street brawls, which reached their climax in Altona, near Hamburg, on 17th July. In a savage encounter between Nazis and Communists 19 were killed and 285 wounded.

The Altona riots gave Papen an excuse to resolve the political deadlock in Prussia, where a Social Democrat-Centre coalition held office without a majority in the Diet. On the grounds that it was unable to maintain law and order, Papen deposed the Prussian government by Presidential Decree, appointing himself as Reich Commissioner for the State.

Meanwhile the election campaign was in full swing, with the Nazi propaganda machine on the top of its form. Again the Nazi vote increased to give them, at the end of July, 230 seats in the Reichstag. They were clearly the largest party, though an outright majority eluded them, as it always did in free elections. Drunk with the prospect of power, the S.A. continued its violent activities, and on 9th August a Communist miner was kicked to death in front of his mother in the Silesian village of Potempa.

Hitler himself felt strengthened by the elections. When he met Schleicher, by arrangement on 5th August, he demanded the Chancellorship for himself and other high offices for his lieutenants. Convinced that Schleicher was amenable, he left the interview in high spirits, having suggested to the General that a plaque be erected to commemorate their historic meeting.

However, Papen also felt his position to be stronger. He was well aware that sympathy for the Nazi party had waned in industrial circles, as a result of the violent socialist opinions, expressed by Strasser, Feder and others, in the last election campaign. Papen also judged, correctly, that Nazism's mass popularity had reached its peak and would henceforth decline. Like most men who obtain power he was in no hurry to relinquish it, and was prepared to deal with Hitler only on his own terms. On 13th August the Fuehrer secured an interview at which Papen and Schleicher offered him the Vice-Chancellorship. In return they witnessed one of Hitler's unbridled outbursts of threatening fury, which horrified them both. Later in the day Hindenburg sent for the Nazi leader and sternly admonished him for his conduct, before dismissing him. At the same time the demands for absolute power he had made were leaked to the press, and probably lost Nazism some support.

Neither side had gained much from these exchanges. The door had been slammed in Hitler's face once more, and Roehm and his henchmen argued strenuously in favour of a *putsch*. But Hitler's nerve and determination had never been stronger. Despite its apparent failure he adhered to his 'policy of legality'. It was the wisest course. Papen was no stronger than he had ever been, and had no alternative but to dissolve the Reichstag and hold fresh elections.

6th November was the date fixed for what proved to be the last major election of 1932. This time the Nazis faced an uphill fight. The word had gone out from Papen, and the flow of industrial funds to the Nazi Party dried up. To make this situation worse, the Nazis felt obliged, a few days before the election, to join the Communists in supporting a transport strike in Berlin, for fear of losing working-class votes. For the first time since 1930 Nazism's popular support fell. The party won only 196 seats, which kept it as the largest single group in the Reichstag, but votes had clearly been lost, on the left to the Communists, and on the right to the National Party. Thus the Nazi position seemed weaker; otherwise the political situation was exactly what it had been before.

Papen undoubtedly felt his position to have improved, with the result that he overplayed his hand. He renewed his offer to Hitler of the Vice-Chancellorship, but this the Fuehrer rejected. Impasse had been reached, and Schleicher once more took up his self-appointed role as kingmaker. He had chosen Papen, believing he would be a pliant instrument with which to construct a right wing coalition including the Nazis. This, the Chancellor seemed loth to do, and Schleicher now urged him to resign, to allow the President the opportunity of consulting all party leaders, in order to resolve the deadlock. Papen was infuriated, but agreed to go, thinking that the consultations would fail, and he himself be restored with greater power. Hindenburg had no wish to lose Papen, but accepted his resignation and his advice to send for Hitler.

Talks began between the President and the Fuehrer on 18th November. Hindenburg offered Hitler the Chancellorship if he could construct a parliamentary majority. Clearly there was no purpose in removing Papen if government still had to be carried on by decree. Hitler demanded the powers Papen had held, and a lengthy correspondence ensued between him and Otto Meissner, which led nowhere. Meanwhile, discussions between Hindenburg and other party leaders produced no result, but Schleicher's fertile mind evolved new variations on his theme of a Nazi alliance.

This time he approached Gregor Strasser with the suggestion that the Nazis should join a coalition in which Schleicher himself was Chancellor. The Party leaders discussed this at a conference in Weimar on 1st December. Strasser and several others were keen to accept the General's offer, but Hitler refused to be drawn. As Goebbels wrote in his diary : 'Anyone can see that the "System" is breathing its last, and that it would be a crime to form an alliance with it at the present moment.'

On the same evening, Papen, Schleicher and Hindenburg also met. Papen proposed that he should resume office and prepare constitutional reform, meanwhile ruling by decree and breaking opposition by force. Schleicher objected that this was unconstitutional, would provoke civil war, and was unnecessary since he, if appointed as Chancellor, could secure a Reichstag majority. Outraged by Schleicher's suggestion, Hindenburg entrusted Papen with forming a new government, but at a cabinet meeting held the following evening Schleicher used his irrefutable argument: the Army no longer had confidence in Papen and could not risk civil war. Papen informed the President of this and, regretfully, Hindenburg requested his resignation. On the same evening Schleicher emerged from his obscurity to become Chancellor of Germany.

General von Schleicher's chancellorship constitutes the final series of events which ended in Hitler's appointment. His conduct left him isolated. No one owed him loyalty, and Papen and Hindenburg hated him. He now had to prove his assertion that he could form a Reichstag majority, since Hindenburg was not prepared to use his emergency powers to help anyone, other than Papen, remain in office. Schleicher's character was fatally flawed, but he was possessed of considerable intelligence. He genuinely disapproved of Papen's willingness to rule by force, since it would not cure existing evils. He assessed accurately the popular force behind the Nazi movement and sought to harness it to the state. What he failed to appreciate was the nature of its *Weltanschauung*.

The new Chancellor began by offering the Vice-Chancellorship to Gregor Strasser, in the hope that he would carry at least some of the Nazi deputies with him. Throughout the year Strasser had been ready to compromise, and he revived all his arguments against Hitler's apparently self-defeating tactics.

As head of the party organization, Strasser was impressed by the recent decline in popular support and knew that radical elements were drifting into the Communist camp. A bitter conflict ensued between him and the Fuehrer, which ended in Strasser resigning all his party offices and taking his family to Italy for a holiday. Whether Strasser could have ousted Hitler from the leadership is not clear. Certainly the movement was desperately short of money and in a demoralized, defeatist mood, but Hitler's personal prestige was enormous, and he rallied his followers in a series of meetings with party officials throughout Germany.

Schleicher, meanwhile, was running into grave difficulties. He pursued a sensible policy intended to deal with the economic situation, but he fell between two stools. His conciliatory approach to labour failed to overcome the distrust the Social Democrats and trade unions felt for him. The Centre would not be reconciled because of his treatment of Bruening, although his intended measures were similar to Bruening's own. Industrialists disliked his treatment of labour. Farmers opposed his reduction of agricultural protection, and the Junkers again raised the cry of 'Agrarian Bolshevism' at his plans for subsidized land settlement in the East.

The impasse was resolved for the last time by none other than Franz von Papen. On 4th January 1933, he and Hitler — two men motivated by nothing save the desire for power — met, by arrangement, at the home of a Cologne banker, Kurt von Schroeder. Circumstances enabled them to rationalize their mutual dislike and concentrate on the hatred they shared for Schleicher. In principle they agreed to form a Nazi-Nationalist coalition, Hitler giving the appearance of one ready to compromise. A newspaper report of their meeting caused some embarrassment, but further contacts were made and, significantly, industry once more began subscribing to Nazism.

Most of the necessary intrigue against Schleicher had to be left to Papen. The latter was well placed. He was on excellent terms with Hindenburg and met him regularly on a social basis. The Nazis concentrated their efforts on the election in the small province of Lippe, and the upswing they achieved in their popular vote probably impressed Hindenburg and Papen.

By 21st January final negotiations began for a Nazi-Nationalist alliance, in Ribbentrop's house at Dahlem, with Goering, always acceptable in moneyed circles, acting as chief Nazi spokesman.

In the course of the following week, Hitler made an important gain in winning the support of Oskar von Hindenburg; this was probably done by blackmail, and Hitler may have threatened to disclose Oskar's part in tax evasion on the presidential estate at Neudeck.

Papen indicated, during negotiations, his willingness to serve under Hitler in a cabinet based on a Reichstag majority. But to achieve this he knew he would have to overcome Hindenburg's dislike of Hitler, and he toyed privately with an alternative scheme to become Chancellor with the help of Hugenberg, in a presidential cabinet, and rule by decree. On his side Hitler indicated his preparedness to enter a coalition, but he was determined to be Chancellor. Plenty of scope was left for bargaining over cabinet posts, and it seems to have been agreed that certain ones, for example the Ministry of Defence, should be reserved for the President's nominees.

From 23rd January to 28th January Schleicher sought emergency powers from the President, but Hindenburg refused, using exactly the same arguments that Schleicher had used to engineer Papen's dismissal. By 28th January the negotiations at Dahlem were sufficiently mature for Papen's purposes. Hindenburg again rejected Schleicher's request for emergency powers, leaving him with no option but to resign. For the third time Papen was entrusted with the formation of a government.

Throughout Sunday, 29th January, the Nazi leaders waited to hear that arrangements had been completed for a full coalition between Papen, Hitler and Hugenberg. They waited, because Papen still dallied with his schemes for making himself presidential Chancellor again. It was from General von Schleicher, making his final bid, whom they heard. His emissary was General von Hammerstein, Commander-in-Chief of the *Reichswehr*. The latter brought warning that Papen might double-cross the Nazis, and suggested a Hitler–Schleicher coalition based on the support of the Army and the Nazis. Hitler's reply was non-committal, and he became more alarmed at the rumour that Schleicher was preparing a military *putsch*. The Berlin S.A., and police battalions with Nazi officers, were alerted to forestall such an eventuality, although it seems unlikely that Schleicher intended to take such action.

In principle, Hitler's fears were justified. Everything had come to hinge on the attitude of the Army. But that was no longer determined by Schleicher. The Army's attitude rested with Hindenburg and General von Blomberg.

The old Field-Marshal personified the military tradition, and could easily suppress a military coup. He had by now agreed to the formation of a Hitler ministry, and had nominated General von Blomberg to serve in it as Minister of Defence. Blomberg was currently adviser to the German delegation to the Disarmament Conference, but had been recalled from Geneva without the knowledge of Hammerstein or Schleicher. If, on his return, he accepted the Defence Ministry, Hitler was practically certain of the Army's support.

Early on the morning of 30th January, Blomberg arrived at Berlin station to be met by Hammerstein's adjutant ordering him to report to the Commander-in-Chief, and Oskar von Hindenburg ordering him to report to the President. It was the latter order that Blomberg obeyed. He was prepared to take office under Hitler. Shortly before noon Hitler was summoned to the Presidential Palace. He emerged as Chancellor of Germany.

CHAPTER SIX

The Nazi Revolution

NAZISM was a revolutionary movement, and its purpose was to destroy the existing order. What would replace it was less clear. Strasser and Feder envisaged a socialist state, Roehm intended to create a huge army, based on the S.A., and under his command. Hitler was concerned to achieve power and, because his will prevailed, the Nazi revolution was simply a struggle for power.

Hitler was already Chancellor, but he sought absolute arbitrary power. Only in general terms did he know or care how he would use it, and to win it was an end in itself. During the election campaign of February 1933 he boasted that he had no programme, and appealed for support only on the grounds that the existing system had failed, and should be replaced.

Nor did the Fuehrer have a set plan for obtaining uncontrolled power. He had become Chancellor as much by the mistakes of others as his own tactics, and he continued to pursue an opportunist policy. He was in the position he had needed in order to overthrow the State from within, the logical conclusion to his 'policy of legality'. But his strength was his unwavering conviction that he would succeed, and his absolute certainty about what he wanted. Others hoped to promote constitutional reform or economic stability, to destroy trade unionism, to preserve catholic schools or establish the dictatorship of the proletariat. They recognized that power was necessary to achieve their ends, but their will to grasp it was a pale shadow of the will of a man who sought power for its own sake.

Hitler's appointment had been conditional on his winning a

Reichstag majority, and only three of the eleven cabinet posts were held by Nazis. Thus Papen had presumed to tame the Party and use it.

To provide a majority entailed drawing the Centre into the Nazi–Nationalist coalition. Monsignor Kaas, leader of the Centre, submitted a list of questions to serve as a basis for talks, but Hitler interpreted them as unnegotiable demands and persuaded his colleagues that, with no agreement possible, elections were necessary. Hugenberg saw the danger of allowing the Nazis to fight an election armed with the power of the state, as they would, since Hitler would remain Chancellor *pro tempore* after the dissolution. But since Hugenberg objected to a coalition with the Centre, and suggested as an alternative an authoritarian régime, Hitler could conveniently ignore him on the grounds that he had promised Hindenburg to seek a parliamentary mandate for his government.

The Nazis entered the election campaign convinced of its outcome. Industry fell into line and contributions came from Krupps, United Steel, I. G. Farben and others. Goering, now Prussian minister of the Interior, purged the State's police and appointed active S.A. leaders to vital posts. An auxiliary force of 50,000 men was raised largely from among the S.A. and S.S. who simply wore white armbands on their party uniforms and provided a veneer of legality when helping their comrades to terrorize Jews and Nazism's political opponents. Even official figures admitted that fifty-one people were killed during the campaign. The Nazis monopolized government controlled radio networks, while their leading orators stormed the country making frenzied speeches.

Seeking to disorganize opposition, the police raided the Karl Liebkrecht House, in Berlin, and an official communiqué described the discovery of plans for a Communist revolution. No concrete evidence was produced, and none was needed after the night of 27th February, when the Reichstag building went up in flames. A young Dutch Communist, van der Lubbe, was accused of firing it, and was later found guilty and executed. The attempt to implicate Communist leaders was a fiasco, and they were released.

PLATE III. Hitler and some of his associates shortly before their accession to power. Left to right (front row), Himmler, Frick, Hitler, General von Epp, Goering. Back row, Martin Nutschmann (Governor of Saxony), Goebbels, Bernhard Rust, later Minister of Education.

It was widely assumed that the Nazis secretly burned the Reichstag to provide grounds for the suppression of the K.P.D., but recent investigation makes it probable that the Dutchman was guilty, as he always avowed.

Whatever the truth, Hitler used the opportunity to persuade Hindenburg to sign a decree of 28th February, which suspended guarantees of individual liberty, allowed the Reich government to assume full powers in States, if necessary, and increased the penalty for crimes like treason, arson and, ironically, grave breaches of the peace. Meanwhile the K.P.D. was allowed to function, in order to split the left-wing vote between it and the Social Democrats.

Despite the means at its disposal, the Nazi Party won only 43·9 per cent of the votes in March. A majority of Germans had voted against it, but more voted for it than for any other party, and, since the Nazi–Nationalist coalition won a Reichstag majority, it is fair to say that the German people had signified their acquiescence in the destruction of democratic government.

Hitler was now able to implement legal revolution. A single law provided the constitutional basis of the Nazi régime, the Law for Removing the Distress of the People and Reich, usually called the Enabling Law. It empowered the government to legislate for four years, without Reichstag consent, including deviations from the constitution, and foreign treaties. Such laws were to be drafted by the Chancellor, and become effective on the day after publication. The Enabling Law, as an amendment to the constitution, required the agreement of two-thirds of the Reichstag, but this was readily obtained. Many Communist deputies were arrested under the law of 28th February, the Nationalists comforted themselves with a clause in the Law declaring the President's powers unaffected, and the Centre satisfied itself with lavish promises from Hitler, and a written statement from Hindenburg that the Chancellor would not use his new powers without consulting him. Many conservatives and *Reichswehr* officers were dazzled by the splendid ceremony held in Potsdam

Garrison Church on 21st March 1933, when Hitler spoke fervently of his loyalty to German tradition.

Two days later the Reichstag met in the Kroll Opera House to confirm the Enabling Law. The Social Democrats alone, to Hitler's undisguised fury, voted against it, an act of considerable courage with the S.A., outside the building, chanting: 'We want the bill — or fire and murder'. Previous chancellors had depended on the President's willingness to sign emergency decrees, but Hitler now had that power himself, with the right to suspend the constitution.

Thus armed, the Nazis launched the policy of *Gleichschaltung*, 'co-ordination', by which vital institutions were brought under Party control.

As early as 9th March the Nazis had seized power by force in Bavaria, where the *Reichswehr* remained neutral on orders from Berlin. Goering already controlled Prussia, and by virtue of the law of 28th February, Nazis were appointed as Police Commissioners in Baden, Saxony and Württemberg. In April *Reichsstatthaelters*, Reich governors, were appointed in each state with power to appoint or dismiss governments and officials, dissolve diets, and publish laws. Hitler replaced Papen as *Reichsstatthaelter* of Prussia. In January 1934 State Diets were abolished and sovereign powers of the states transferred to the Reich. The states retained a formal existence but the dual system, originating in 1871, had been swept away.

Rival political parties were quickly suppressed. Goering's Prussian State Police, the Gestapo, went into action, and concentration camps were opened at Dachau and elsewhere to receive political undesirables. The Democrats and People's Party, who had lost most of their support to the Nazis, dissolved themselves. Social Democrats, Centre and K.P.D. found their buildings, newspapers and funds confiscated and their leaders under arrest. Even the Nationalist offices were occupied, and Hugenberg, bowing to the storm, dissolved his party. On 14th July a new law declared the Nazi Party the only legal party in Germany and provided penalties for attempting to organize any other. Papen, Hugenberg and the others, who jobbed Hitler to power, had intrigued in a conventional manner. They were quite unprepared for a movement which, armed with a single law, applied the methods of gangsterism to political life.

While the Fuehrer conducted his political revolution, the rank and file pursued their own aims. Violence was blatantly employed by the S.A., who established 'bunkers', in the cellars and warehouses of big cities, where people were beaten or held to ransom for every vicious reason from greed to sadism. Simultaneously there was a scramble for jobs and positions as mayors, civil servants, company directors and so on. Many of those who climbed on the bandwagon were opportunists, the *Maerzgefallene*, who joined the Party only in its hour of triumph.

The radical wing renewed its attack on capitalism. Otto Wagener, head of the Economic Department, sought control of the employers' associations, Adrian von Renteln, leader of the Combat League of the Middle Class Tradespeople, tried to weaken the power of the big department stores, Walther Darré, now Minister of Agriculture, demanded reduction of agrarian debts and interest rates, and Feder advocated fulfilment of the socialist points in the party programme. Roehm and his henchmen became involved in a quarrel with the Army, which saw its preeminence threatened when the street gangs came to power.

It seemed possible that this revolutionary wave would not abate until every institution had been remodelled, but it threatened Hitler's power revolution and so there were limits beyond which he was not prepared to let it go. He had no sympathy with socialism, and he was no economist, but he knew enough not to jeopardize the economic foundations of the state, and announced bluntly on 6th July: '. . . We must not dismiss a good businessman . . . especially not if the National Socialist who is to take his place knows nothing about business.' Still less could he risk offending the Army. Its professional skill would be required for rearmament, and probably war. More important was the fact that it took its oath of loyalty to the President, and in that significant respect Hitler's power was not yet absolute. Hindenburg was ailing, and when he died Hitler intended to absorb his power and, with it, the allegiance of the Army. Only if he supported the Generals against the S.A. could he do this, and the matter became more urgent after April 1934, when Hitler and Blomberg were confidentially informed that the President had only a short time to live. Many officers favoured a monarchial restoration, and so did Hindenburg. That they would carry it out unless Hitler met their requirements was not to be doubted.

The economy was placed under reliable, orthodox direction. Dr. Schacht, an ardent Nazi sympathizer, was already President of the Reichsbank. The director of Germany's biggest insurance company, Dr. Schmitt, became Minister of Economy and Trade, Krupp, von Bohlen and Thyssen retained control of the employers' associations, the Combat League was dissolved and no more heard of Darré's schemes. Talk of corporate economic development was forbidden in the Party.

It took longer to deal with the S.A. Roehm described the popular impulse for change as the 'Second Revolution', and he represented all the discontented elements of which it was compounded. The S.A. were the *Alte Kämpfer*, the old fighters, who had not won their expected rewards. Roehm sympathized with the radicals, criticized the suppression of the Trade Unions in 1933, and disliked Hitler's tyrannical ambition. Above all he was determined that the para-military force he had created should become the core of an expanded army which he would command.

Hitler may not have decided until the last moment how to resolve the problem. For several months he tried to conciliate both sides. Shortly after becoming Chancellor he assured the Generals of his intention to strengthen their position, and on 20th July civil jurisdiction over military courts was annulled. In several speeches Hitler tried to reassure the Army during the second half of 1933. On the other hand, Roehm, as Chief of Staff of the S.A., was brought into the cabinet, and in February 1934 state pensions were provided for party members injured during the 'national struggle'. But when Roehm pressed for consolidation of all armed forces, under himself as responsible Minister of

State, Hitler declined to support him against the Generals' implacable opposition.

As relations between the S.A. leaders and High Command deteriorated, Hitler must have known which side he would support if a choice became inevitable. The Army was essential to increase his power, the S.A. could only hinder him. Early in 1934 the Army leaders agreed that Hitler should succeed Hindenburg, while in return they were promised the monopoly of bearing arms. Whether this pact was concluded at the War Office in February, or negotiated on the *Deutschland* during manoeuvres, is not clear; that it was made is beyond dispute.

What happened in the councils of the S.A., the Nazi leaders, and the Generals during April, May and June 1934 will never be clear. It is beyond reasonable doubt that the documentary evidence was destroyed, and certainly many of the protagonists were. The official version, given by Hitler on 13th July, was that Roehm contacted Schleicher and they agreed to execute a *putsch* which would make Schleicher Vice-Chancellor and force Hitler to consummate the 'Second Revolution'. Gregor Strasser and General von Bredow were alleged to have been implicated, and overtures made to the French ambassador for help. The *putsch* was imminent on 30th June, and was forestalled only by the drastic measures taken on that day. Almost certainly this was an apologia compounded of exaggeration, half-truth and lies.

Early in June Hitler may have been continuing his conciliatory policy, or attempting to lull Roehm into a sense of false security. He had a long talk with Roehm, of which little is known, and agreed to attend a conference of S.A. leaders, to discuss the future of the movement, at Wiessee near Munich, on 30th June. The S.A. was ordered to go on leave for the whole of July, and Roehm himself went on sick leave on 7th June. Until half-way through the month Goebbels held furtive meetings with Roehm, which he seems to have reported to Hitler, while the latter may have made a last effort to bring Strasser back into political life.

Meanwhile Roehm's avowed enemies were undoubtedly more decisive. Goering, now a *Reichswehr* general to his great delight, sided with the Army, hoping to become its supreme commander and therefore regarding Roehm as a rival, while Himmler, chafing with resentment at the subordination of the S.S. to the S.A., and with ambitions to create a police empire, was also eager to be rid of Roehm. In April, Goering unexpectedly appointed Himmler as effective head of the Gestapo. General von Reichenau, a strong Nazi sympathizer, and now driving force behind the Minister of War, met Himmler several times and it is a fair inference that they planned a swift end to the 'Second Revolution'.

If Hitler still hesitated about giving Himmler and Goering a free hand, the events of 17th June to 21st June must have helped him to decide. Papen unexpectedly reasserted himself by making a speech at the University of Marburg on 17th June, which was outspokenly critical of the 'Second Revolution' and the abuse of Nazi propaganda. The speech was drafted by Edgar Jung and Herbert von Bose, who worked in the vice-chancellory, and Erich Klausener, who represented Christianity and the decent element in German conservatism. Although Goebbels hastily suppressed printed copies of the speech, it circulated widely, and Papen was acclaimed on his next public appearance. Hitler's relations with the traditional German right were at the cross-roads, and on 21st June, when he visited Hindenburg at Neudeck, Blomberg informed him that, unless the present tension was relaxed, the President would declare martial law and hand power to the Army. The future of the Nazi régime was at stake.

Meanwhile, rumours of an S.A. *putsch* circulated without any supporting evidence. Sepp Dietrich, head of Hitler's S.S. bodyguard, produced a list of people the S.A. intended to shoot. Its veracity is suggested by the fact that General Fritsch and Beck, to whom he showed it, were at the top. Circumstantial evidence suggests that the S.A. leaders were far from intending a *putsch* on 30th June, the alleged date. Karl Ernst, the Berlin leader, went on his honeymoon that day, and Roehm, with his circle of young men, was on holiday in Bavaria awaiting the Fuehrer's arrival at Wiessee.

Certainly there was unrest in the S.A., but largely occasioned by fear that the Army would move against it. Such suspicion was not unfounded; in the last week of June all army leave was cancelled, Roehm was expelled from the Officers' League, and an article, signed by Blomberg, appeared in the *Voelkischer Beobachter*, making the Army's position clear.

Almost certainly the S.S. had contrived to set the Army and the S.A. at each other's throats, while making their own preparations to eliminate their enemies. Hitler must have known what was afoot, but it is a matter of opinion whether he led Goering and Himmler, or was persuaded by them, to take action on 30th June. Some of the Generals also knew, but with their equivocal code of honour, merely provided arms, transport and barracks for the murder squads of the S.S.

On 29th June Hitler's period of gestation or indecision, whichever it was, ended. He flew from the Rhineland to Munich, arriving at 4 a.m. A column of cars raced to Wiessee, Roehm and his lieutenants were dragged from their beds and taken to the Stadelheim Prison, where Dietrich's men acted as firing squads.

In Berlin Goering and Himmler had gone into action on 29th June, and executions continued throughout the weekend. Karl Ernst was caught near Bremen, and other S.S. leaders were executed at the Lichterfelde Cadet School, where Goering's personal police were quartered. Schleicher was shot in his home, and Bredow on his own doorstep. Strasser was executed in prison, and Bose, Jung and Klausener were shot, substitutes for Papen, whose friendship with Hindenburg saved him even from Goering.

Many an old score was levelled that weekend. Gustav von Kahr, seventy-three and now retired, was found in a swamp, hacked to pieces. Father Bernhard Stempfle was shot 'trying to escape'. It can only be assumed that his 'crime' was to know too much about Hitler's enigmatic love affair with his own niece, Geli Raubal, in the nineteen-twenties. In Munich Willi Schmid, a music critic, was murdered in mistake for a local S.A. man. His widow eventually received a state pension and the advice from

Rudolf Hess, the Fuehrer's deputy, to think of her husband as a martyr in a great cause.

On 3rd July a statement in the *Voelkischer Beobachter*, drafted by Reichenau, gave essentially the same account of what happened as Hitler gave ten days later. Thus the Army faked justification for what it had abetted, including the murder of two of its own. It has been argued that the Generals dug their own graves in 1934, but the Officer Corps survived, as it would not have done had Roehm come to power. The S.S., whatever Himmler's aspirations, never achieved what Roehm had intended, and failed to infiltrate the High Command. An S.S. military establishment was permitted, but it remained small and dispersed until 1942. Only after defeat did the High Command find itself hamstrung and faced with an expansion of the *Waffen* S.S., and by then it was too late for the S.S. to become a serious rival, and it was only so in internal matters of administration and discipline, while the Army generals retained control of S.S. divisions in the field. The Army's mistake had been to accept Hitler in the first place, and its later humiliations were not the result of the Blood Purge of 1934, but of events which were then unforeseeable.

Himmler emerged stronger from the Roehm purge. It was an important step towards the S.S. gaining control of all the police organs in Germany. Viktor Lutze, nominally Roehm's successor, willingly played a subordinate role, and the S.S. began to establish itself as a state within a state.

The Fuehrer had won absolute power. On 3rd July it was decreed that the measures taken to suppress the *putsch* had become law for defence of the State in an emergency. Henceforth any crime committed by the Nazis was, *ipso facto*, legal. Nine days later the legal officers of the Reich were informed that henceforth its law was the will of the Fuehrer.

On 2nd August Hindenburg died and the Army kept its bargain. Hitler became President and to him personally all ranks vowed: 'I swear by God this holy oath: I will render unconditional obedience to the Fuehrer of the German Reich and People, Adolf Hitler, the Supreme Commander of the Armed

Forces, and will be ready as a brave soldier to stake my life at any time for this oath.' Hitler had already broken his promise, and permitted the formation of an S.S. armed division, obedient to Himmler.

On 19th August the German people were invited to approve, by plebiscite, Hitler's assumption of power as Fuehrer and Reich Chancellor. Of 45,500,000 voters 95·7 per cent went to the poll. Thirty-eight million, or 89·9 per cent of the votes cast, said 'yes'. Four and a half million said 'no' and 870,000 papers were spoiled. The four and a half million should not be forgotten, but the majority was impressive. The Nazi revolution had received popular confirmation.

CHAPTER SEVEN

Nazi Germany

THE Weimar Republic was defective, but it was based on a rational constitution and a comprehensible pattern of administration. The government of the Third Reich almost beggars description. Authority overlapped, functions were duplicated, and the whole was vitiated by the interminable intrigues and insatiable ambitions of the Nazi leaders.

Presiding over confusion, held together by terror, was Hitler. Physically he was unimpressive, with a lank forelock falling across his forehead and a Charlie Chaplin moustache. 'I go', he said, 'the way Providence dictates with the self-assurance of a sleep walker.' His intuitive approach to politics could not be better summarized, but he was a master of using events, and his sense of timing and opportunity remarkable. Devoid of scruple himself, he trusted no one and rejected all expert opinion when it clashed with his own, believing that insuperable will would remove all obstacles from his path.

A talented actor, he dominated personal relationships and interviews. He was capable of infinite self-dramatization, posing as one shamefully wronged, and justifying himself in a fury of righteous indignation. Apparently overcome with blind rage he would, in an instant, calm down and resume talking in a normal voice. On occasion he manifested great personal charm, and many witnesses have recorded the magnetic quality of his personality, connected, it appears, with eyes of almost hypnotic power.

He possessed a remarkable, though fallible, memory for detail, which he used to impress his generals, when he poured out streams of statistics at military conferences. Many of them later proved inaccurate, but the immediate impression of mental concentration was what Hitler wanted to give.

He was one of the most compelling orators of all time. His voice was harsh, he often repeated himself and strayed from the point, but his delivery carried such emotional impact that German audiences were entranced and even sceptical foreign journalists were impressed at the time.

The Fuehrer had little personal life and Eva Braun, his mistress from 1932, was hardly known even in Germany, and neither she nor any other woman was the Pompadour of the Third Reich. He neither smoked nor drank, and became a vegetarian, but he took no exercise and had a passion for cream buns and sweets. A hypochrondriac, he suffered from indigestion and insomnia so that his entourage was regularly obliged to sit up into the early hours of the morning listening to the Fuehrer reminisce about his years of struggle, or lecture on any subject that took his fancy. Two of his outstanding characteristics were his capacity for intense, lasting hatred, and his vanity. Members of his court flattered his most banal remark, and only Roehm and Gregor Strasser ever refused to conform. In the end he became convinced of his own infallibility and gripped by megalomania, and in that sense was mad. No one better illustrates the truth of Acton's dictum that absolute power tends to corrupt absolutely.

To the end, the decrees that he issued were 'legal'. The constitution of 1919 was never formally abrogated, and new decrees were based on the Law for the Protection of the People and the State of 28th February 1933, and the Enabling Law, which was prolonged every four years by a specially summoned Reichstag. Hitler promulgated his decrees through four chancellories, administrative departments; those of the President, the Chancellor, the Party and the Fuehrer. The last two, run by Martin Bormann and Hans Lammers, became the most important.

Serious cabinet discussions ended in 1933, and after February 1938 the cabinet never met, but individual members possessed authority to issue decrees which, with Hitler's consent, became law. Many cabinet responsibilities were delegated to special agencies. Thus Schacht became Plenipotentiary for War Economy, and Goering, Delegate for the Four Year Plan. Some forty-two other distinct executive bodies functioned under the authority of the Fuehrer.

Routine matters of government bored Hitler, who lacked the temperament to work long regular hours, and his lieutenants were free to build their own empires so long as they did not challenge the will of their Fuehrer. Indeed he encouraged this, as he had in the nineteen-twenties, as a means of preventing cabals against him. Thus, until 1938, Neurath was officially Foreign Minister, but Rosenberg ran a rival Party Foreign Affairs Department, and Ribbentrop his personal Foreign Bureau. The situation in military intelligence, where several competing agencies existed until 1944, was far worse.

Most powerful of all these empires was Himmler's S.S. The tiny force which had begun as Hitler's bodyguard never became a state within a state, as its leader intended, but its ramifications were immense by 1944. The *Waffen* S.S. functioned as soldiers, the Death's Head Units ran the concentration camps; as *Reichs-fuehrer* S.S., Himmler controlled the complex police forces of Germany, and the S.D., originally the S.S.'s security service, acquired control of all military intelligence. Thousands of civilian employees belonged to the General S.S., and hundreds of important officials to the honorary S.S. Among its activities were German archaeology, ancestral research, collecting skulls of Jewish–Bolshevik commissars, running baby farms, the investigation of astrology and the cultivation of medicinal herbs. It ran schools, a mineral water plant, foreign night clubs, a publishing house and a porcelain factory. Most of these bore no relation to the rest, and they constituted the ramshackle empire of a man who was undemonstratively but quite clearly mad.

We have already seen how the autonomy of the federal states was destroyed, and between 1933 and 1935 municipalities suffered the same fate. Hitler himself appointed the burgomasters of Berlin, Hamburg and, after 1938, Vienna; the Reich Minister of the Interior appointed the mayors of towns with a population over 100,000, and the *Reichsstatthaelters* those of towns below that figure.

At all levels the Reich was administered through the *fuehrer-prinzip*, by a confused bureaucracy possessing none of the efficiency usually attributed to the German people. It survived Hitler for seven days, and it is unlikely that it would have lasted much longer, even without the circumstances of overwhelming military defeat.

Working conditions were closely regulated. The Trade Unions were destroyed in the first wave of *gleichschaltung*, to be merged in the German Labour Front, led by Robert Ley. A Law Regulating National Labour, January 1934, defined an employer as 'leader' of a commercial or industrial enterprise, and employees as 'followers'. Employers possessed the sole right, subject to state interference, to make decisions concerning the enterprise. Employers were responsible for the welfare of their employees who, in return, owed what was euphemistically termed 'faithfulness'. The Labour Front, regularized by a law of 1934, theoretically replaced trade unions, but it included employers and professional men, as well as wage earners and salaried staff. It was closely linked with the Party, and most of its officials belonged to the S.S. Its aim was 'to create a true social and productive community', in which everyone did the maximum of work.

Various decrees after May 1934 restricted freedom of movement and employment. Over a million farm workers ignored these and moved to the towns during the nineteen-thirties, but industrial workers were effectively controlled. After February 1935 each worker had to possess a workbook containing the record of his qualifications and experience. Without it he could not be employed, and, since it was held by his employer, to change jobs became impossible without the employer's consent. In 1938 industrial conscription was introduced, everyone was directed to his place of work and absentees were fined or imprisoned.

Wages were regulated by trustees appointed by the Labour

Front, and no machinery existed for consultation with labour. Normally fixed according to the wishes of employers, wages were held down by the state after 1936 when some armaments manufacturers tried to raise wages to attract skilled men. Day rates in many industries did not provide a living wage, so that long hours on piecework were unavoidable.

During the nineteen-thirties the level of wages fell, and, despite the sharp decline in unemployment, the total share of wages in the national income fell by 3·3 per cent between 1932 and 1938, while the share of dividends and profits rose by 9·2 per cent. Admittedly total income from wages rose by 66 per cent, but total income from investments and profits rose by 146 per cent. Certainly the amount of his wages a German took home was reduced. In some cases up to 35 per cent of gross wages disappeared in taxes, sickness, unemployment and disability contributions, and obligatory subscriptions to various Party charities. Labour Front dues were high, particularly when it grew into a typical Nazi bureaucracy which spent a quarter of its income on internal administration.

Not only work, but also leisure, was controlled through *Kraft durch Freude*, Strength through Joy, an organization allied to the Labour Front. Members of the Front were provided with inexpensive sea-voyages and ski-ing holidays, regimented to the last detail. Sports, in which seven million people competed annually, were extensively organized. Cheap tickets to the theatre, concerts and the opera were available to working men, and two hundred adult education institutes were taken over, and Nazi ideology added to their curricula. The subsidies were, inevitably, more apparent than real, since 10 per cent of Labour Front dues went to *Kraft durch Freude*.

Hitler once asserted that in the Third Reich every German girl would find a husband, and, in an equally expansive mood, after coming to power, he decided that every German workman should own a motor-car costing only 990 marks. The Labour Front was put in charge of building this *volkswagen*, the people's car, designed by Dr. Porsche with the Fuehrer's personal assist-

ance. The production factory was built at Fallersleben, largely
financed by a scheme under which workers contributed a mini-
mum of five marks each week, until they had paid 750, whereupon they received an order number for a vehicle to be delivered
as soon as the balance was paid and the car produced. None ever
was, and after 1939 the factory turned over to the production of
military equipment.

Dr. Schacht was the architect of economic recovery. Public
works, for example on the autobahns, were expanded, and
government credit and tax relief given to firms which increased
capital expenditure. Thus unemployment figures were reduced
to one million in 1936. The currency was so skilfully manipulated
that it had 237 different values at one time, and profitable barter
deals were arranged with foreign countries. Rising employment
increased home consumption and a stabilized economy once
more attracted investment. These factors, rather than massive
rearmament, promoted recovery, certainly until 1936. The in-
auguration, in that year, of the Four Year Plan, under Goering's
direction, began the trend towards a war based economy. Schacht
had been appointed Plenipotentiary for War Economy in 1935
but had not yet achieved much and, believing that to make
Germany ready for war in four years would prove too great a
strain, resigned in 1937. The Plan led to the reduction of imports,
stricter control of wages, prices and dividends, and the opening of
factories for synthetic rubber and textiles, and the Hermann
Goering factory to make steel from low grade ore. Even so it has
been shown that armaments expenditure was not so great as was
once thought, while bureaucratic confusion and the monumental
ignorance of economics which Goering shared with his Fuehrer
must have hindered progress.

The Third Reich was not the *laissez-faire* paradise some business
men may have hoped for. One-fifth of all small firms were closed
by a law dissolving those with a capital of under 160,000 marks,
and new ones could not be floated on less than 800,000 marks.
In contrast huge cartels were strengthened and new, compulsory
ones organized. Scores of existing business and trade associations

were forced into a complex structure at the head of which was the Reich Economic Chamber. Beneath it were seven national economic groups, twenty-three economic chambers, one hundred chambers of industry and commerce, and seventy chambers of handicrafts. In the same field there operated the Minister of Economics and the Delegate for the Four Year Plan, each with a variety of subordinate offices. Bribery was commonplace as businessmen sought out key officials from whom to obtain orders, raw materials, planning permission, or the means to circumvent one of innumerable regulations. Nevertheless profits were good, and the restriction on dividends above 6 per cent evaded by reinvestment in the same enterprise. Finally, employers were no longer faced with increased wage demands or strikes.

Germany's agrarian economy was in ruins in 1933, and farmers burdened with debt. The Nazi programme had promised land reform, confiscation of land for common purposes, abolition of interest on farm loans and an end of land speculation. Only the last point was fulfilled, and the extensive Junker estates east of the Elbe remained untouched while the small farmer was closely regulated. Farms of up to 308 acres were declared hereditary, inalienable and indivisible. They could neither be foreclosed upon nor mortgaged. Thus the farmer won security but was effectively bound to the soil. His work was supervised by the Reich Food Estate of which Darré was Reich Peasant Leader. Although the organization raised agricultural prices, the farmer found that his machinery and fertilizers were also costing more, while the attempt to make Germany self-sufficient in food was unsuccessful.

Education was reorganized by Dr. Rust, former *Gauleiter* of Hanover, who had been dismissed from his teaching post in 1930 for mental instability. Textbooks were re-written, curricula revised, and *Mein Kampf* became the 'infallible pedagogical guiding star'. Teachers were required to join the appropriate party organization, sent on intensive ideological courses, and eventually had to have served in the S.A. or the Hitler Youth. Defined as civil servants, they were subject to racial laws and obliged 'to defend without reservation the National-Socialist state'.

Universities were stultified establishments preaching racial nonsense. Rectors were nominated by Rust, and lecturers were appointed only after attending an ideological course from which they emerged with a favourable report on their political reliability. Membership of Students' Unions and the National Socialist Association of University Lecturers was compulsory. History was reduced to absurdity, and a distinction made between German mathematics and inferior varieties. Professor Rudolfe Tomaschek of the Dresden Institute of Physics wrote that modern physics was a Jewish invention for the destruction of Nordic science, and held that true physics had been created by the German spirit. Professor Lenard of Heidelberg denied that science was international, and insisted on its racial quality.

Not only did academic standards decline, but between 1933 and 1938 the number of undergraduates was halved, and the number enrolled in Institutes of Technology was reduced even more. Not only was the lack of qualified scientists and engineers felt in industry, but national defence was jeopardized, and the Germans had only themselves to blame when the Allies won the race to split the atom during the war.

Orthodox education had never impressed Hitler, and more emphasis was placed on the *Jungvolk*, or Hitler Youth, as a means to indoctrinate the young. Before 1933 the Nazi youth organizations had been insignificant compared to the Reich Committee of German Youth Associations with over ten million members. In 1933 Baldur von Schirach, an immature young man who led the Hitler Youth, two of whose ancestors had signed the American Declaration of Independence, became Youth Leader of the German Reich. He confiscated the property of the Youth Associations and began to expand the *Jungvolk*, which was the only legal organization of its kind after 1936, when Schirach, formerly subordinate to Rust, became directly responsible to Hitler.

Boys joined the junior section of the movement at the age of six and, having passed tests in nazified history, athletics and camping, graduated, at ten, into the *Jungvolk* where they remained until eighteen. It was a uniformed organization giving systematic instruction in camping, athletics, ideology and military training. Members passed, at eighteen, into the Labour Service.

From ten to fourteen girls were *Jungmaedel*, and undertook similar training to boys, while from fourteen to twenty-one they belonged to the *Bund Deutscher Maedel*. At eighteen they performed a year's service on farms. Their camps were frequently near those of the Labour Service and the number of pregnancies which resulted was a scandal to all save the true believers. It was emphasized to the B.D.M. that motherhood was their racial duty, within marriage if possible, but outside it if necessary.

By early 1939 four million young people remained outside the movement and they were conscripted into it. Parents had always been liable to imprisonment if they restrained their children from joining, and they were now threatened that their children would be sent to state orphanages if they failed to obey the law.

The purpose of the Hitler Youth was to stamp the Nazi *weltanschauung* on each new generation. The Adolf Hitler Schools, the Political Institutes of Education, and the *Ordensburgen* existed to train the inner élite.

There were ten of the first type, which took promising members of the *Jungvolk* at the age of twelve, gave them six years of Spartan training to fit them for party leadership, and automatically qualified them for university entrance. The Political Institutes, thirty-one in number, of which three were for women, were staffed by the S.S. and cultivated the martial spirit and Nazi ideology.

The *Ordensburgen*, Order Castles, dear to the heart of Himmler, were based on the medieval Order of Teutonic Knights, with its absolute obedience to the *Ordenmeister* and devotion to the conquest of Slav lands. Only the most successful pupils of the Adolf Hitler Schools and the Political Institutes were chosen to attend them. There were four castles and students attended each in succession. The first emphasized 'racial science' and Nazi ideology, the second, athletics, mountaineering and parachuting, and the third political and military instruction. The fourth castle, at Marienburg, on the Polish frontier, had once been a stronghold of the Teutonic Knights, and political and military training was focused on *Lebensraum* and Germany's right to expand into the East.

No other faith or ideology could hope to escape persecution in such an atmosphere, unless its adherents were prepared to compromise with their own ideals. Unfortunately the Christian churches were. The Nazi view of Christianity is indicated in an unfulfilled scheme, drawn up by Rosenberg during the war, for a National Reich Church. This was to exterminate orthodox Christianity, replace priests by 'National Reich orators', the Bible by *Mein Kampf*, and the Cross by the swastika.

Hitler, as usual, was more realistic. He was prepared to allow the churches a formal existence so long as they refrained from questioning his authority. Shortly after becoming Chancellor he paid tribute to the Christian faith and expressed his desire to seek accord between Church and State. The first practical result of this policy was a Concordat with Rome, signed on 20th July 1933. The Vatican undoubtedly hoped to secure protection for the faithful in Germany, but in the following years Catholic Youth organizations were proscribed, priests and nuns imprisoned on false charges, and even the confessional violated by the Gestapo. The encyclical 'With Burning Sorrow' of March 1937 accused the Nazis of fundamental hostility to Christianity, but by then Hitler no longer needed the temporary prestige the Concordat had given to the Nazi régime. In any case, the tone of the encyclical had little effect in Austria, when the *Anschluss* took place in the following year. The Austrian bishops signed a declaration that 'we . . . will, in future give [the work of the National Socialist movement] our blessing, and will instruct the faithful accordingly'. Cardinal Innitzer, Archbishop of Vienna, wrote to the *Gauleiter* of Vienna that the declaration had been signed 'voluntarily and without coercion'.

The Protestant churches, too, welcomed Nazism at first. Most of Germany's forty-five million Protestants were Lutheran. In general the pastors had been hostile to the Republic and were not

D

troubled by its collapse. By 1933 there was in existence an avowedly Nazi wing of the Protestant faith, the German Christians Faith movement. Led by Ludwig Mueller, an army chaplain, it approved of racial doctrines, the *fuehrerprinzip*, and aimed at the establishment of a single 'Reich Church'. Three thousand pastors belonged to it. In direct opposition to it was the Confessional Church, while most Protestants remained uncommitted.

In 1933 representatives of the Protestant churches drew up a constitution for a Reich Church, which the government approved. Dispute arose over the election of the Reich bishop. Hitler wanted Mueller elected, but many influential pastors favoured Friedrich von Bodelschwingh, an eminent divine. Intimidation produced a German Christian majority in the electoral synod and Mueller became Reich bishop, but he proved incapable of imposing even outward conformity. Shortly after his election, at a German Christian rally, Reinhardt Krause proposed abandonment of the Old Testament and revision of the New Testament in accordance with National Socialist requirements, but so strong was the opposition that Mueller had to disavow him.

Early in 1934 Martin Niemoller, a former U-boat captain, who had welcomed the advent of Nazism, saw the light and became head of the Confessional Church, which declared itself the only legitimate Protestant church in Germany. Several hundreds of its pastors were arrested, but the breach was not healed, and Hitler appointed as Minister for Church Affairs a moderate Nazi lawyer, Hans Kerrl. The latter appointed a committee under the widely respected Dr. Zoellner, to evolve a compromise.

The Confessional Church co-operated, but continued to assert its independence and, in May 1936, presented a courteous but critical memoranda to the Fuehrer. Immediately the Confessional Church found many of its pastors arrested and its funds confiscated, and Zoellner resigned his post in despair, early in 1937. In June that year Niemoller preached a courageous anti-Nazi sermon at his Dahlem church, was arrested, and imprisoned. In March 1938 he was tried on various charges, heavily fined and sentenced to seven months in prison. Having already served a longer sentence than this, he was released, only to be taken into 'protective custody' by the Gestapo, and until 1945 he remained in Sachsenhausen and Dachau.

With the arrest of Niemoller and his followers, opposition collapsed. Late in 1937 Bishop Marahrens obliged Kerrl by announcing that 'The National Socialist conception of life . . . is obligatory on German Christians . . .', and he ordered all pastors in his diocese to swear a personal oath of allegiance to Hitler. By the end of 1938 most Protestant clergy had done the same.

A typically complicated machine, consisting of party and state elements, existed to control literature, the arts, entertainment and mass media. Joseph Goebbels, Minister of Propaganda, directed this. In addition to his ministry, he controlled the Reich Chamber of Culture which delegated its functions to seven sub-chambers, one each for fine arts, music, literature, the press, the theatre, radio and films. A party stalwart was at the head of each sub-chamber; for example, Max Amman ran the press, and its decisions had the force of law. All who worked in these fields were obliged to belong to the appropriate chamber.

The symbol of Nazi treatment of culture was the bizarre episode of the burning of the books on the evening of 20th May 1933. On Unter den Linden, opposite Berlin University, and in several other cities, huge bonfires were lit, and books unacceptable to Nazism were thrown into the flames by hysterical students. The works of Germans like Thomas Mann, Einstein and Erich Maria Remarque, of foreigners including H. G. Wells, Freud, Zola and Proust, and many others were ceremonially burned that night. Practically no German literature of merit was published during the Nazi era, and most writers followed Thomas Mann into exile.

Music suffered little since it has little political significance except by the association of individual works with particular events or movements. Musicians were left to practise their art if they avoided opposition to Nazism. Wilhelm Furtwaengler continued his career as a conductor, and Richard Strauss was, for a time, president of the sub-chamber of music. The works of Men-

delssohn and Hindemith were forbidden since they were Jews,
but otherwise the Third Reich enjoyed the rich heritage of German music. The theatre also retained high standards while
classical plays were performed, although the offerings of Nazi
dramatists, including Goebbels, were of poor quality and played
to small audiences.

As an artist of hitherto unrecognized merit, the Fuehrer himself took an interest in purging Germany of modern art. The
works of Cézanne, Picasso, Van Gogh and many others vanished
from the walls of German galleries. To replace them, an exhibition of Nazi paintings was held, in 1937, in the House of German
Art in Munich, partly designed by Hitler. In another part of the
town Goebbels organized an exhibition of the 'degenerate' art
from which the Fuehrer had rescued his people. To their credit,
the people of Munich were so ungrateful that they preferred it
to the exhibition of Nazi painting, and the embarrassed Minister
of Propaganda closed it after a few days.

The press was controlled by daily conferences at which the
editors of Berlin newspapers and correspondents of the provincial press were given detailed verbal and written instructions
about what to print and how to express it. One of Germany's
greatest papers, the *Vossiche Zeitung*, was put out of business in
1934 after 230 years. Other former liberal papers, like the
Frankfurter Zeitung, survived, perhaps in an attempt to impress
the outside world where they were widely respected, but their
editorial policy was Nazi.

So uniform was the press that circulations fell rapidly and
Goebbels and Amman called for a more lively approach. The only
editor to take them seriously, Ehm Welke of the *Gruene Post*,
was quickly taken into protective custody. So many publishing
firms were taken over by *Eher Verlag*, the Party publishing house,
that it became one of the wealthiest in the world.

The Nazis monopolized broadcasting after 1933, when they
automatically assumed control over the Reich Broadcasting
Corporation. Goebbels quickly made it a vital instrument of
propaganda, but it was not until the war years that tuning to

foreign wavelengths became a serious offence. The cinema was also used for disseminating Nazi ideas, but the films were so bad that people either stayed away, or jeered at them to such an extent that Frick, Minister of the Interior, issued a warning against 'treasonable behaviour on the part of cinema audiences'.

To be a Jew in the Third Reich was to be an outcast. The Nuremberg Laws of 1935 deprived them of their citizenship and reduced them to the status of 'subjects'. Marriage, as well as extra-marital relations, was forbidden between Jews and Aryans. By the end of 1938 the Jews were disbarred from public office, the civil service, the law, medicine, the stock exchange, teaching, journalism, agriculture and the entertainment industry. Supplementary decrees to the original laws continued until 1st July 1943, when Germany was held, incorrectly, to be free of Jews, and they were declared outlaws, wholly at the mercy of the police and with no legal status.

Throughout Germany many grocers, bakers, chemists, dairies and hotels refused to serve them. Many civic boundaries were marked by signs forbidding or discouraging the entry of Jews. After the *Anschluss* Austrian Jewry was subjected to similar persecution and the Jewish Emigration Office, which was to conduct the 'Final Solution', was established in Vienna under Adolf Eichmann.

Also in 1938 some ten thousand Jews were deported to Poland, in conditions soon to become commonplace, and in November the first official pogrom took place after a young German Jew had assassinated an official at the embassy in Paris. Ultimately it was Hitler's responsibility, but it was directed by Reinhard Heydrich, and carried out by his S.D. with the co-operation of Nazi Germany's variety of police forces, on the night of 9–10th November, soon after the Fuehrer's court had finished its annual celebration of the Beer Hall *Putsch*. The instructions issued by Heydrich made it clear that Jewish property was to be destroyed, but not looted, the police were not to hinder demonstrators, and that wealthy Jews were to be arrested. Exact figures are unknown, but over a thousand Jewish synagogues, shops and homes were burned, and thousands of Jews arrested. Murder had neither been ordered nor forbidden. Probably over one hundred Jews were killed that night but no serious action was taken against those responsible; only those Nazis who had so far forgotten their Aryan blood as to rape Jewesses were expelled from the Party and tried in civil courts for offences against the Nuremberg Laws. Following this 'Week of Broken Glass', as it was called, the Jews were eliminated from economic life and ordered as a community to defray the cost of damage done during the riots, and pay a thousand million mark fine.

Justice had not always been impartially administered before 1933, but afterwards justice, as an abstract ideal, disappeared completely. Judges had to show their political reliability and belong to the League of National Socialist German Jurists, which was frequently lectured by Hans Frank, the Party's legal adviser since the nineteen-twenties. He made it clear that judgments should be handed down, in accordance with how the Fuehrer would decide, and 'compatible with the National Socialist conscience of the German people'.

So incensed was Hitler at the failure of the German Supreme Court to convict all the defendants at the Reichstag Fire trial that a new court, the *Sondergericht*, was established to try political offences. It consisted of three judges and no jury, and counsel for the defence had to be approved by the Party's legal department. The lawyers who acted for Erich Klausener's widow, when she sued the state for damages, before the *Sondergericht*, found themselves incarcerated in Sachsenhausen until they withdrew the suit.

Even more sinister was the *Volksgerichtshof*, or People's Court. Of its seven judges, five were Nazis, there was no appeal from its decisions, and it normally sat *in camera*. Hitler, and for a time Goering, had the right to quash any criminal proceedings, and Rudolf Hess was empowered to take 'merciless' action against any defendant he thought to have been dealt with too leniently for offences against the Fuehrer, the Party or the State.

It is impossible to draw a clear line between the functions of the judiciary and the police in Nazi Germany. The police network was ubiquitous and inspired terror among the civil population which was, perhaps, its prime purpose. Almost total destruction of the records of the Gestapo — its most notorious arm — makes it impossible to judge how professionally competent it was. Almost certainly it was inefficient. This is not to imply that it failed to arrest thousands of people, but so wide were its powers, and so compliant the courts, that it had no need to collect much evidence of guilt, or to be sure which of the many suspects it arrested was involved in the case in hand.

In its final form the Nazi police system was the usual confusion of party and state apparatus. The Weimar Republic had been heavily policed, and each state was responsible for its own force. In Prussia, which constituted two-thirds of Weimar Germany, the State Minister of the Interior had ultimate responsibility for the police, which was run for him by a Chief of Police who commanded the following units. The Kripo was a conventional criminal investigation department in plain clothes, and the Stapo the equivalent of the English Special Branch, dealing with political security. The Orpo, or Order Police, were organized on military lines, carried small arms, lived in barracks, and were used as riot squads. The Schupo and Gendarmerie were conventional constabularies policing the towns and countryside, and in addition there were Fire, Railway and Water Police.

By 1933, when Goering became Prussian Minister of the Interior, Artur Nebe, who was secretly a member of the S.S., although civil servants were forbidden to belong to political parties, was in charge of Kripo. On Himmler's recommendation Goering appointed a high-ranking S.S. officer, Kurt Daluege, as Chief of Prussian Police, and his own nominee, Rudolf Diels, was put in command of Department 1A of Stapo, which became the Gestapo. It established headquarters in a former art school in Prinz Albrecht Strasse. With Diels's help, Goering's purge of the Prussian police was carried out.

Meanwhile, in Munich, Himmler, head of the S.S., had appointed a cashiered naval officer, Reinhard Heydrich, to establish an internal party security service, the *Sicherdienst*, S.D., and secured control of the political police in the states other than Prussia. Himmler aimed at securing control of police throughout the Reich. Heydrich abetted him, while pursuing his own ambitions to control both civil and military intelligence and security services, and Daluege was their foothold in Berlin.

The intrigues and vendettas in the Berlin police forces in 1933 are almost incredible. Nebe walked round his own department with his hand on his pistol, and walked upstairs close to the wall, in order to reduce his visibility as a target from the landing above. On one occasion Daluege, Nebe and certain of their associates considered throwing Diels out of a third-storey window, an S.S. detachment once raided Diels's flat, Diels arrested a local S.S. Captain, and members of the Gestapo arrested each other so frequently that no one thought it odd. Despite all this, Prinz Albrecht Strasse was becoming a place of terror for the German public. In the course of 1934, as we have seen, Goering conceded effective control of the Gestapo to Himmler, and Heydrich established S.D. headquarters in Berlin at the same time.

Under Hermann Mueller, who replaced Diels, and remained as head of the Gestapo until 1945, its activities flourished. In 1936 it was placed above the law, since there was no appeal from its decisions. Thus Niemoller, among others, was taken into 'protective custody', which meant consignment to a concentration camp.

The same year saw many important developments. Himmler was formally appointed as Chief of German Police, and began his campaign to detach the Gestapo from the State and place it under the S.S., thus enabling the party, and his own unit of it in particular, to dominate the whole police system. The police were now divided into two: Orpo, and Sepo, security police including Kripo, the Gestapo, and, in effect, the S.D. Daluege became head of Orpo, and Heydrich of Sepo. Inspectors from each branch were appointed in every military district to co-operate with the Army Commander and *Gauleiter*, while the S.S. leader in each territorial division of S.S. organization became Chief of

Police for that area. The term Gestapo was extended to cover the unified political police of the whole Reich and Prinz Albrecht Strasse was its H.Q.

During 1937 Himmler's decisions, as *Reichsfuehrer S.S.*, were given the validity of ministerial decisions, and all members of Kripo and the Gestapo were required to join the S.S. Thus the Gestapo, a state organization, was effectively brought under control of the S.D., a party organization. The situation was formally recognized when the Gestapo and Kripo were placed under the Main Security Office of the S.S., henceforth known as the Reich Main Security Office, R.S.H.A., run by Heydrich, and after his death in 1942, by Ernst Kaltenbrunner, who was responsible to Himmler.

It contained seven Amts, or bureaux; the first two were concerned with personnel and administration, Amt III was S.D. (home intelligence); Amt IV, the Gestapo; Amt V, Kripo; Amt VI, S.D. (foreign intelligence); Amt N was concerned with technical communications; and Amt VII with scientific exploitation. Many of these bureaux had further sub-sections; Amt IV, the Gestapo, had eleven before the outbreak of war, and others were added afterwards. Orpo, less important, remained outside this complex. Himmler as Chief of Police was responsible for it, but the Ministry of the Interior had some hand in its affairs. In 1943 the situation was simplified when Himmler became Minister of the Interior.

In practice the activities of these components of the Nazi police system are inseparable. At the post-war Nuremberg trials attempts to allot responsibility proved futile. The only broad distinction possible is that the R.S.H.A. operated outside the concentration and death camps, which were guarded and administered by special units of the S.S. What happened outside was largely the work of the R.S.H.A. of which the S.D. and Gestapo were the most important elements. Neither was a large organization; there were only 3000 men in the S.D., and the Gestapo, even at its height, had only 40,000 employees including clerks and women typists; but probably over 100,000 part-time spies were used, even before the war, thus ensuring that any unguarded word reached the ears of authority, enabling it to take action, often unnecessarily, but giving an impression of omniscience.

It should be emphasized that the Gestapo and the S.D. were not merely Germany's equivalent of M.I.5 or the F.B.I., nor were the differences solely in the methods employed. The political arm of the police in democratic countries is a defensive instrument to protect the existing situation which has been freely sanctioned by the electorate. The Gestapo was an instrument of terror and aggression intended to impose the Nazi will on its opponents.

The brutal methods of the Nazi secret police are world notorious. Flogging was the only torture its captured members admitted to, but the evidence of its victims shows that identical items of unpleasantly ingenious equipment were used wherever it operated. It is a fair inference that many of the cruelties practised by the Gestapo were standard procedure. The ultimate terror it had at its disposal was to consign its victims to a concentration camp.

The first concentration camps were often S.A. barracks where Jews and others were held to ransom, but when the régime was established such places were closed, and regular camps were opened. Control of them was given to the S.S. and guard duty was done exclusively by the Death's Head units, while hardened criminals, selected for their strength and brutality, acted as overseers and block commanders, the notorious *prominenten* or *kapos*. The first camp, at Dachau, was commanded by Theodor Eicke, who later commanded the S.S. Camp Inspectorate. By 1939 the main ones were Dachau, near Munich; Sachsenhausen, near Berlin; Buchenwald, near Weimar; Ravensbrueck (for women), in Mecklenburg; and, after 1938, Mauthausen, near Linz. Probably no more than thirty thousand prisoners were in these at any one time, until 1938, but by spring 1939 there were 279,168. The early camps were not humane — inmates could be hung for loitering or shot for refusing to work — but mass extermination, 'medical research', and the other evils, were not perpetrated until wartime.

The first experiment in mass murder took place in nursing homes. Provision for compulsory sterilization in certain cases was made in 1933, but in 1939 Hitler determined on euthanasia for incurable mental defectives. Party leaders seem to have been unhappy about this measure being applied to Germans, and Hitler issued a secret decree through the Fuehrer's Chancellery to two ranking Nazis, Philip Bouhler and Karl Brandt, to put the scheme into operation, although it is clear that the party aristocracy knew of what was happening and the matter involved a typical network of intrigue at high level. Six main institutes were used and a number of lesser ones. Those murdered included children, but how many people died, and whether or not they were all incurable defectives, will never be known, but for two years the systematic extermination of German people was carried on.

Nazi Germany was, beyond dispute, a dictatorship, but whether it was also a totalitarian state is questionable. Certainly its authoritarian, single party structure contrasts with the liberal democratic concept in which the state's role is limited, and certain functions are left to individual decision. It extended its influence over private as well as public life, and enforced complete submission to its demands, but there was never the complete centralization of power and authority which would exist in the true totalitarian state. Even when Germany was fighting for survival, the S.S. competed with the military authorities in the development of guided rockets. Inefficiency, and the existence of so many personal empires at high level, prevented the Nazis from achieving complete totality of the state. None the less, the effect of their régime on the German people was much the same. Craftsmanship, professional life, religious faith, the bearing and rearing of children, and all other significant human activities, were perverted to serve the glory of the Reich. Few, if any, human activities ought to be pursued without regard for their social consequences, but it is the merit of democracy that it

allows them to be pursued also for their own intrinsic worth.
Nazism denied the existence of any value other than its service.

How far the German people loyally abetted this retreat from
the truth is a vexed question. Most Europeans remember one or
both of the World Wars, and are often ready to believe that the
Germans readily followed Hitler, while the Germans and their
apologists often use Hitler or the S.S. as their alibi, or beg the
question by criticizing the Allies for their failure to help the
German opposition, or by arguing that the Allies were equally
barbarous in their use of the atomic bomb.

It still remains for some future historian to reach a balanced
estimate of the involvement of the German people with Nazism.
There was opposition, and an attempt will be made later to
assess its significance. Ultimately it failed, as it would not had
most Germans been active in it. Thus it is a reasonable inference
that the majority were at least acquiescent.

Increased employment did much to reconcile wage-earners
with the régime. Industrial conscription at least gave security,
since no employer could easily dismiss directed labour, and low
wages, regularly paid, gave a higher standard of living than
many had endured in the depression years. *Kraft durch Freude*
offered a variety of recreation beyond the means of most wage-
earners anywhere else in Europe of the nineteen-thirties.

The middle class submitted. Every school-teacher and most
protestant ministers and university professors took a personal
oath of loyalty to Hitler, and accepted the exclusion of the Jews
from professional life. Gerald Reitlinger has shown that the
euthanasia campaign, although facilitated by the existence of S.S.
Guard Units and medical officers, was carried out largely by
civilian medical staff and nurses. He makes the further point
that they did their work without any knowledge of the secret
decree which authorized it. The police, too, accepted the new
régime easily. Many members of Kripo and the Gestapo were
policemen of the Weimar era who accepted their duties without
complaint, and both Reitlinger and Edward Crankshaw have
emphasized how much they were helped by thousands of Ger-

mans. Every police force has its informers, but the Gestapo seems
to have had a large number.

Over fifteen million parents allowed their children, as members
of the *Jungvolk* before 1939, to take an oath of loyalty to the
Fuehrer. Perhaps the physical well-being of the children eased
their consciences. William Shirer, the American historian and
journalist, noted the contrast between the fit appearance of
German soldiers and the pallid undernourished rankers of the
B.E.F., victims of twenty years' neglect.

A great number of Germans were indifferent to the fate of the
Jews, and those who were concerned argued that they could do
little to help. This may have been true, but it is significant that
pressure of public opinion contributed to the cessation of the
euthanasia campaign. The inference is that Jews were not worth
the risk, taken by Clemens von Galen, Archbishop of Muenster,
when he preached in public against euthanasia of Germans.

German conservatism, which had done so much to bring the
Nazis to power, submitted to the new régime. After the Marburg
speech Papen accepted the post as Ambassador to Vienna,
Neurath remained at the foreign office, and many other career
diplomatists stayed at their posts to put their experience and
training at the disposal of the Nazis. The industrialists were
generally satisfied, business improved, and labour troubles ended.
Later many industrialists were not averse to using slave labour
and some willingly constructed equipment for extermination
camps.

The supine attitude of the Officer Corps became clear in 1938.
By then it had accepted the swastika as part of its insignia, and
presumably approved much of what had happened. It was
authoritarian, and had excluded Jews from its ranks long before
1933. Above all, the breaching of the Versailles Treaty allowed
it to begin open reconstruction of a large army. In 1935 some
reorganization took place. Blomberg became Minister of War and
Commander-in-Chief of the *Wehrmacht*, the Armed Forces.
Beneath him the Army, Navy and Air Force, each had its own
Commander-in-Chief and General Staff. Hitler's title of Supreme

Commander of the *Wehrmacht* was certainly not nominal, but the Army retained considerable control of its own affairs.

In 1938 the Generals received a major public humiliation when Blomberg and General von Fritsch, the Army Commander-in-Chief, were dismissed. As in the Roehm Purge, the precise role of certain participants is open to different interpretations, but the main lines are clear. Both officers had been sceptical of the speed at which Hitler wished to be ready for war, and Fritsch had never concealed his contempt for the Nazi movement. By 1938 Hitler was ready to be rid of them, and took his opportunity. The unholy alliance of Goering and Himmler was ready to spring the trap, part of which Himmler and Heydrich had been preparing since 1935, Goering because he aspired to Blomberg's post, and Himmler because he hoped to incorporate the Army into his expanding S.S. empire.

In 1938, Blomberg, a widower, married his young secretary, Erna Gruhn. The Berlin police promptly unearthed a dossier, which may or may not have been faked, showing her to have a record of prostitution. Via General Keitel and Goering, it reached Hitler, who was furious, probably because he had been a witness at the wedding, and Blomberg was dismissed. Goering may have known of the dossier some time before. In view of his motive in these events it is suggestive that he advised Blomberg, who sought his advice, to marry Erna Gruhn, a commoner — hence Blomberg's doubt — and even disposed of a rival by posting him to South America.

Almost simultaneously with Blomberg's fall, another police file appeared, this one certainly the unpleasant concoction of Heydrich and Himmler. It purported to show Fritsch had been guilty of homosexual offences and, since 1935, had paid blackmail to conceal his guilt. In the presence of Hitler, Himmler and Goering, he was faced with the alleged blackmailer, a degenerate habitual criminal, Hans Schmidt. Hotly, he denied his guilt and refused to resign, demanding to be tried by a Court of Honour, but Hitler ordered him to go on indefinite leave.

In the tense atmosphere of the next few days Berlin seethed

with rumours of a military *putsch*, particularly after a pre-
liminary investigation by the Army and Ministry of Justice proved
to the last detail that Fritsch had been framed, so that his exonera-
tion before a Court of Honour was inevitable. On 4th February
1938, the crisis was resolved. A new decree reorganized military
high command. The War Ministry was abolished and replaced by
the High Command of the Armed Forces, *Oberkommando der
Wehrmacht*, O.K.W. At its head was Hitler, and beneath him the
sycophant Keitel as Chief of Staff. It was announced that Fritsch
had resigned on health grounds, which every senior officer knew
to be untrue. Sixteen senior generals were relieved of their commands and forty-four others transferred. General von Brauschitsch
replaced Fritsch as Army Commander. At the time he was seeking
a divorce, but as it was for the purpose of marrying an ardent
Nazi, Charlotte Schmidt, the Fuehrer overlooked the latest irregu-
larity to obtrude in the private lives of his generals. Indeed he
apparently did what he could to expedite matters.

The Generals had lost another opportunity to unseat Hitler,
particularly in view of the diminished strength of the S.A. since
1934, and the small size of the armed S.S. Even in the face of
their own humiliation they did nothing, who had always claimed
to be guardians of the Reich, to rescue it from a movement
which would lead it to destruction.

At the same time Hitler purged the Foreign Office, Neurath was
replaced by Ribbentrop. Papen was replaced in Vienna, and two
conservative diplomats, Herbert von Dirksen and Ulrich von
Hassell, were recalled from key embassies in Tokyo and Rome.
In this epilogue to the Nazi revolution Hitler had acquired what
power remained to those who had thought to offer him a share.

CHAPTER EIGHT

The Expansion of Hitler's Empire

LATE in 1942 the whole of Europe except Sweden, Switzerland and the Iberian Peninsula was directly under Nazi control, or indirectly under its influence, while the German armies had overrun Russia roughly as far east as a line drawn from Leningrad through Stalingrad to the north-east shores of the Black Sea. The Mediterranean islands from Crete to Sardinia, and the North African coast opposite, were also under Axis occupation. This remarkable extension of Nazi power was the result of an oppressive and unscrupulous foreign policy.

After consolidating his power in Germany, Hitler became absorbed in foreign affairs and military planning, and interpretation of his policy in these fields is controversial.

The view taken here is that he held a number of ultimate objectives with unswerving consistency, but had no preconceived plan for attaining them. Rather he relied on his intuition, sense of opportunity and flair for timing. The risk of war was implicit in his objectives, and he knew it. Before 1939 he correctly judged the risk to be slight, but in September of that year was probably surprised to find himself at war with France and England. After that his judgment was increasingly at fault, and he gravely underestimated the consequences of attacking Russia and declaring war on the U.S.A. Only if the rest of Europe had continued indefinitely to pursue an unrealistic policy towards Germany could the Second Word War have been averted. In that important sense it was Hitler's war.

Hitler's aims were the revision of the 1919 settlement in Germany's favour, creation of the Greater Reich and, above all, expansion to the east in pursuit of *Lebensraum*. Subsidiary aims were to secure an Italian alliance and an understanding with Great Britain. Revision of Versailles meant regaining European territory lost in 1919, in particular to Poland and France, and the establishment of Germany's freedom to re-arm without reference to anyone else. The creation of the Greater Reich involved not only the *Anschluss* with Austria, but the incorporation of any area inhabited by racial Germans irrespective of its historical separation from Germany. *Lebensraum* could, in practice, mean only the subjection of Soviet Russia. An understanding with Italy proved relatively easy to achieve, and the Rome–Berlin Axis was established in 1936, but Britain remained a puzzle to Hitler. He never fathomed Britain's disinclination to take strong action against Germany, before 1939, combined with an unreadiness to co-operate. He wavered between hopes for an alliance with Britain, contemplating military action against her, and dismissing her as of negligible importance. Even after the outbreak of war his attitude to her was ambivalent.

For the first five years Hitler was preoccupied with re-arming and freeing Germany from the restrictions of 1919. The risk of armed intervention had to be minimized until this had been accomplished, and foreign suspicion allayed. The opportunity was also taken to forge the Rome–Berlin axis, sign a naval agreement with Britain and the Anti-Comintern Pact with Japan.

To the Dusseldorf industrialists, in 1932, Hitler had declared that 'the primary necessity is the restoration of a sound national German body-politic, armed to strike'. Very soon after becoming Chancellor he told certain generals that they faced the dangerous period of rearmament when France might 'fall upon us', and emphasized to the cabinet that military requirements would be a basic consideration for the next few years. Hitler proceeded to argue the justice of Germany's case in public, playing on the feelings, common in England, that Versailles had been unfair as well as impolitic. It was, but Hitler had no intention of stopping at revision. He used dislike of Versailles as a means to his own ends.

In the famous Peace Speech, delivered to the Reichstag in May 1933, he argued that Germany alone had disarmed, and was ready to do so completely if others did the same. He stressed his dislike of war, which he reiterated in an interview given to the *Daily Mail* in October, and told the correspondent of *Le Matin*, in November, that he had renounced all claims to Alsace-Lorraine.

He plausibly explained Germany's departure from the Geneva Disarmament Conference, and the League of Nations, in October 1933, as the result of continued denial of equality to Germany, and even held a plebiscite on leaving the League as earnest of his good intentions.

More startling was the Pact with Poland. Relations with Poland were shot through with a sense of grievance on one side and deep distrust on the other, and there were a number of minor war scares in 1932 and 1933. But the Army insisted on its unreadiness to fight even a defensive campaign and Poland was offered a non-aggression pact. Fearing that Germany might now act outside the framework of the League, the Poles accepted and a ten-year Pact was signed in January 1934. Hitler had postponed a final settlement with Poland until a convenient moment, and could meanwhile parade his virtue in solving one of Europe's most dangerous problems.

Meanwhile clandestine rearmament was continued from the Weimar period, but neither this nor the policy to be based upon it could be accomplished within the limitations of Geneva and the League. Hence Germany broke with them in October 1933, no sanctions were applied, and Hitler's gamble had succeeded. When Britain and France sought renewal of disarmament negotiations, Hitler replied that these could be based only on the recognition of Germany's right to raise an army of 300,000 on the basis of conscription and short-term service. Agreement was not reached, despite a lengthy exchange of notes during the winter of 1933–4, but increases in German's military expenditure were made public in March 1934, and the western powers were launched on the policy of appeasement.

By early 1935 it was clear that Britain and France were ready to concede Germany's right to re-arm, in return for her adherence to some scheme of mutual security in the east.

Hitler was undecided how to respond until the publication of a British White Paper in March 1935, announcing increased armaments and criticizing German rearmaments. On 9th March the existence of the *Luftwaffe*, the German Air Force, was officially announced. Three days later the French doubled the period of conscript service and reduced enlistment age — mainly to overcome the problem of the low birth-rate between 1914 and 1918 — and on 16th March Hitler announced the introduction of conscription to build up a peace-time army of thirty-six divisions, 550,000 men. In May the Reich Secret Defence Law was issued and, after the remilitarization of the Rhineland in 1936, plans proceeded more quickly.

By 1939 the Army had thirty infantry divisions, four of them fully motorized, five armoured divisions, four light divisions, twenty-two machine-gun battalions and nearly three hundred anti-aircraft batteries. Since 1933 the Germany Navy had put into service two battleships of 26,000 tons, and two even larger were being built, two armoured cruisers of 10,000 tons with four others near completion, seventeen destroyers and forty-seven U-boats. The *Luftwaffe*, created entirely since 1933, had 260,000 men, with twenty-one squadrons. Such were the forces behind Hitler's diplomacy in 1939.

The Versailles Treaty had established a demilitarized zone, thirty miles deep, in the Rhineland, which had been confirmed by the Locarno agreements of 1925 when the Belgo-German and Franco-German frontiers had been guaranteed by Italy, Britain and the countries immediately concerned.

After violating the 1919 agreement in March 1935, Hitler's next logical step was to remilitarize the Rhineland on 7th March 1936. A pretext was provided by the Franco-Soviet Pact of May 1935 which, said Hitler, introduced an 'element of legal insecurity' into Locarno, while Mussolini's attack on Abyssinia provided the opportunity. The Stresa Front, created when the Italian, French and British governments issued a declaration at

Stresa, in April 1935, condemning German rearmament and affirming loyalty to Locarno, was in disarray. In the middle of February Hitler had decided to reoccupy the Rhineland, taking as his occasion the ratification of the Franco-Soviet Pact, whenever it occurred.

For Hitler this was a serious decision. Talks between the Duce and Hassell in January indicated that Italy was seeking a *rapprochement* with Germany and the collapse of Anglo-Italian co-operation, but he feared that Italy might help France in exchange for France refusing to adopt sanctions against Italy in the Abyssinian affair, and not until 3rd March, when Hassell obtained written confirmation, was Hitler certain that Mussolini would not oppose him. The British attitude worried Hitler until the end. In fact the British government had made it clear to France that they would not act. The French attitude was never in doubt. France was quite aware of Hitler's intention, as he knew, but he did not know that she would not act alone. Thus the entry of a few troops into the Rhineland on 7th March was less of a gamble than Hitler may have thought. Success favourably altered his whole position, for the last step in the re-establishment of Germany's military independence had been accomplished. No internal activity could provoke French intervention, hence the acceleration of rearmament.

The advent of the Axis was perceptible early in 1936. Austria had prevented a *rapprochement* between Nazi Germany and Fascist Italy, but the Duce's Abyssinian adventure not only isolated him, but left him without the means to continue his former role as Austria's protector, and he was content to view the Austro-German agreement of 1936 as a solution to the Austrian problem. In the same month he incautiously became involved in supporting General Franco in the Spanish Civil War, which ruined any chance of revived co-operation with Britain or France. Hitler had written in *Mein Kampf* of the need for an Italian alliance, for which he was prepared to exclude the German South Tyrolese from the Reich, and he was diverted from what seems to have been his intention to seek an understanding with Britain, in the late summer of 1936. Contacts between Rome and Berlin resulted in the signing of a secret protocol in October 1936. Neither side was obliged to help the other in the event of a European war, but they agreed to follow a common policy in Spain and South-east Europe. As yet there was no military alliance, but the ties between the Axis powers grew stronger and the road ran straight from 1936 to the Steel Pact of 1939.

Meanwhile, Japan had been considered as a possible ally. Her activities in Asia might divert Russia from Europe, and the Soviet Government was not only the ultimate enemy, but had recently signed agreements with France and Czechoslovakia. Despite some fear that Japanese activity in China might threaten important German economic interests there, the Anti-Comintern Pact was signed in November 1936. It provided for internal defence against the activities of Comintern, the Communist International, and each contracting party agreed to adopt benevolent neutrality towards the other in the event of attack by the Soviet Union. In November 1937 Italy adhered to the agreement.

Hitler's policy towards Britain was uncertain during these years. In a speech to the Reichstag on 21st May 1935, he emphasized his willingness to limit German naval power to 35 per cent of that of Britain. The British government responded with alacrity and in June an agreement was signed.

It has recently been argued that by the end of 1937 Hitler had turned against Britain. Evidence for this includes the memorandum, drawn up by Colonel Hossbach, of a military conference between Hitler and his generals, held on 5th November 1937. The Hossbach memorandum is a controversial document, but it certainly appears from other evidence that Hitler was in an anti-British mood at that time.

The year 1938 saw a quickening of the pace in Hitler's policy. The conference of 5th November 1937, and the removal of the last traces of open conservative opposition early in 1938, suggest that Hitler was prepared to move more quickly, but the annexation of Austria was, in a sense, forced upon him before he had expected it. Not that he was averse to the *Anschluss* with Austria.

Its accomplishment illustrates both his will to achieve an objective and his opportunism.

The not unreasonable idea of the *Anschluss*, uniting the German-speaking people of Germany and Austria, had blossomed in the nineteenth century. Bismarck had rejected it in 1866, but it persisted, for example in the programme of Schoenerer's party. The dissolution of the Habsburg Empire during World War I removed the greatest obstacle to it, but France insisted on its being specifically forbidden in the 1919 settlement. Not until 1931 was it actively revived in a projected Austro-German customs union, which was defeated by French opposition with Italian and British support.

From the summer of 1932 Mussolini adopted a unilateral policy of preserving Austria, and, in return, expected Engelbert Dollfuss, her chancellor, to introduce essentially fascist measures, and join Italy's close relationship with Hungary.

Hitler's coming to power aggravated the situation since, in contrast to his general policy, he aimed at a speedy consummation of the *Anschluss*. This was because the Austrian Nazis were an integral part of the German movement, which implied that Austria should, like Germany, be nazified. Hitler also believed that the Dollfuss government would soon collapse. It was based on an uneasy alliance between the Fatherland, a patriotic, non-party organization, formed by merging a number of political groups, including Dollfuss's Christian Socials, and the *Heimwehr*, a fascist organization. Hitler prevented German tourists going to Austria, launched a bitter radio propaganda campaign against her, had Nazi leaflets dropped in Austria from aeroplanes, and appointed Theodor Habicht to direct disruptive party activities there.

Dollfuss sought British, French and Italian support, being loth to rely only on Mussolini in case Italian occupation was substituted for an enforced *Anschluss*. Britain and France agreed to put pressure on Berlin, but Mussolini refused, preferring instead to act as Austria's sole protector, and, at the same time, seek German friendship. This wrecked any chance of coercing Hitler, but Italian influence in Austria grew. Early in 1934 Dollfuss realized that Anglo-French support was unlikely, and tied himself closer to Mussolini by accepting the Rome Protocols dealing with economic relations between Italy, Hungary and Austria.

Mussolini's influence was not as great as he believed. His connection with Dollfuss and Stahremberg drove Fey, the other member of the ruling triumvirate, into intriguing with the Austrian Nazis. A meeting between the Fuehrer and the Duce did nothing to ease the tension, and the Austrian Nazis, deciding force was the only solution, launched an abortive *putsch* in July 1934. Dollfuss was murdered, and Italian troops moved to the Brenner, but the Austrian government itself restored the situation. Hitler had given the rebels no help, but had known of the intended *putsch* and believed, on Habicht's evidence, that its success was assured. He was furious at the failure and Habicht's deceit. Henceforward, he decreed, an evolutionary policy was to be adopted, and the highly respectable orthodox catholic, Papen, was sent as Minister-Extraordinary to Vienna.

Kurt von Schuschnigg replaced Dollfuss. He was disinclined to rely on Italy and sought an accommodation with the Austrian Nazis, now shorn of their extremist element, without any definite result. Meanwhile, Mussolini had become involved in Abyssinia and was drawing closer to Berlin. He indicated his willingness to see increased German influence in Austria, and in March 1936 virtually told Schuschnigg to come to terms with Hitler. Not without reluctance, Schuschnigg indicated his readiness to reach a *modus vivendi*, and the Austro-German Agreement of July 1936 was the result. Germany recognized Austrian independence and promised non-intervention in her internal affairs. Schuschnigg agreed to follow a foreign policy parallel to Germany's, and to introduce members of the so-called national opposition into his government. This included the Nazis and other groups with Pan-German ideas.

The Agreement marks the end of Italo-German conflict over Austria, and, with the creation of the Axis, Austria was Hitler's field. Schuschnigg foresaw the danger, but withdrawal of Italian help left him defenceless. The main German lever in the Agreement was the promise to appoint nationalists, not necessarily Nazis, to the Vienna cabinet, and the appointments of Edmund Glaise-Horstenau and Guido Schmidt were the first results. Schuschnigg could not, however, afford to offend the Fatherland Front too deeply by negotiation with the nationalists, and tried, for some months, a policy of appeasing the Reich and being firm with the Austrian Nazis, but this came to nothing and he was obliged to seek conciliation with the Nazis. Nothing significant emerged from this except the appointment of Arthur Seyss-Inquart as the government's contact-man and negotiator with nationalist circles. He was not a Nazi but sympathized with them.

Meanwhile the Agreement was not working well. The German government and Seyss-Inquart were eager to revive negotiations for a customs union, but Schuschnigg proved evasive, and contacts between Goering and Schmidt late in 1937 suggested different viewpoints. In fact Schuschnigg saw the Agreement as the final act of appeasement, Hitler as a step towards the *Anschluss*. The Hossbach memorandum suggests that, by November 1937, he was ready to contemplate using force against Austria, although possibly not until as late as 1945. His emphasis on force was probably to overcome the reluctance of the Generals to accelerating the rearmament programme, and he acknowledged that he still hoped for a peaceful solution to the Austrian problem.

Sensing the imminent collapse of the Agreement, Papen suggested to Hitler and Schuschnigg, in January 1938, that they should confer. Schuschnigg was unenthusiastic, but on learning that Hitler was willing, agreed rather than offend the Fuehrer. Almost immediately Hitler became absorbed in the Blomberg-Fritsch affair, and on 4th February Papen was recalled from his post. He promptly reminded Hitler, who had forgotten, of the proposed meeting, and it was arranged that Schuschnigg should come to the Berghof, Hitler's mountain retreat in Berchtesgaden, on 12th February. Meanwhile Schuschnigg had agreed to a scheme negotiated by Zernatto, his State Secretary, and Seyss-Inquart, for co-operation between the Fatherland Front and the National-Nazi opposition. The *Punktationen*, as it was known, provided that Seyss-Inquart be arbiter on Nazi affairs and for Austro-German military co-operation. There was to be an anmesty for imprisoned Nazis and several were to be given office. It was agreed in principle that Seyss-Inquart should become Minister of the Interior and Public Security.

Unknown to Schuschnigg, these terms had been conveyed to Hitler before he met the Austrian chancellor. Hitler knew exactly how far Schuschnigg was prepared to yield, hence the bullying manner he adopted throughout their talks. The terms of their agreement, dictated by Hitler, were those of the *Punktationen* and Glaise-Horstenau's appointment as Minister of the Armed Forces. They were to be implemented by 15th February.

Schuschnigg began to do as he had been told while Hitler, still pursuing a long-term policy, tried to check resurgent Nazi violence in Austria. Schuschnigg, trying to stem the tide, then tried his last gamble, which had the effect of provoking the *Anschluss* well before Hitler had anticipated it. He announced on 9th March that a plebiscite would be held on the *Anschluss* question on 13th March.

After hesitating for a day Hitler set his military staff improvising plans for the invasion of Austria, and gave the Nazis their freedom of action. He instructed Seyss-Inquart to demand postponement of the plebiscite and made it clear that German military occupation was the alternative. Seyss-Inquart was given a draft telegram to send requesting such intervention. Schuschnigg called off the plebiscite at 2 p.m. on 11th March. Immediately German demands were increased to Schuschnigg's replacement by Seyss-Inquart. Schuschnigg resigned, but President Miklas refused to appoint Seyss-Inquart until at about midnight, under pressure of armed insurgents, he yielded. Meanwhile, after hours of vacillation, Hitler had issued the order for the military occupation of Austria at 8.45 p.m., and was confirmed in his decision by a message from Philip of Hesse, his special envoy to Italy, indicating that Italy would remain neutral. Hitler still seems to have insisted that the occupation take place on the basis of a request from Vienna. Seyss-Inquart had no desire for military invasion and did not comply. Eventually, Wilhelm Keppler, Hitler's contact-man in Vienna, telephoned the erroneous message to Berlin : 'Seyss-Inquart agrees', which satisfied Hitler's desire to preserve appearances.

Having won power when Miklas yielded, neither Seyss-Inquart nor the Austrian Nazis wished to lose it. But the new chancellor's request that German troops be held back was ignored and they crossed the frontier at dawn on 12th March. At this stage Hitler seems to have intended to establish an Austro-German union in his own person, but realizing its feasibility he decreed the annexation of Austria as a province of the German Reich on 13th March. This was later ratified by plebiscite. In view of Hitler's plausible appeals to the principle of self-determination it should be noticed that annexation preceded the plebiscite.

The *Anschluss* was achieved almost against Hitler's will. Confident of Austria's inability to maintain stable government he had adopted an evolutionary policy, but Schuschnigg's decision to hold a plebiscite precipitated a crisis in which Hitler eventually discovered he could risk annexation. His success must have impressed upon him how gradual methods could be accelerated by threats and armed force.

After the *Anschluss* Hitler turned quickly to his next objective, Czechoslovakia. Aware of their danger, the Czechs had allied with France and Russia, but France was committed to appeasement, while Poland and Rumania were unlikely to afford passage to Soviet troops marching to the aid of Czechoslovakia. The existence of three and a quarter millions of Germans in the Sudetenland provided Hitler with the pretext he required. Throughout the crisis of 1938 the ostensible issue was the position of this minority, obscuring Hitler's intention of destroying the Czech state. From 1935 the Sudeten Nazi Party, led by Konrad Henlein, was subsidized from Germany. The Czech government sought an accommodation with its German minority, but after March 1938

Henlein pursued the policy, made in conference with Hitler, of being dissatisfied with any concession offered to him.

By May, Hitler was encouraged by Anglo-French pressure on Prague to meet the Sudeten requirements, and on 20th May Keitel sent him the first draft of Operation Green, plans for war with Czechoslovakia in certain circumstances. Quite unexpectedly the Czech government ordered partial mobilization on the same day and a week-end crisis ensued. It passed, but left Britain and France regarding President Benes as having committed a provocative blunder. His action infuriated Hitler, who changed the opening sentence of the directive Operation Green to 'It is my unalterable decision to smash Czechoslovakia by military action in the near future'. 1st October 1938 was the latest date.

Throughout June, July and August tension increased. Attempts were made to provoke Poland, Rumania and Hungary into seeking territorial concessions from Czechoslovakia, and military preparations continued despite the opposition of Ludwig Beck, Army Chief of Staff, who feared war with the West. It was expected that Hitler would make a statement at the Party Rally in September, and London and Paris, failing to see beneath the surface, urged Prague to reach agreement with Henlein. Chamberlain despatched Lord Runciman as mediator, but Henlein won his sympathy while continuing to avoid any settlement with Benes.

Hitler's awaited speech came on 12th September. It contained nothing concrete, but it broke the unsteady nerves of Chamberlain and Daladier, the French Premier. On 15th September the British Prime Minister flew, on behalf of both governments, to meet Hitler at Berchtesgaden. He agreed to seek means of separating the Sudetenland from Czechoslovakia, and Hitler not to undertake precipitate action.

During the next week German military preparations continued, a Sudeten *Freikorps* was raised, the Slovak People's Party was prompted to demand Slovakian autonomy and Warsaw and Budapest to demand plebiscites in Polish and Magyar areas of Czechoslovakia. Chamberlain worked to secure British, French and Czech agreement to proposals which he handed to the Fuehrer at Godesberg on 22nd September.

The Sudetenland was to be transferred, without plebiscite, to Germany, and Czechoslovakia was to cancel her French and Russian treaties and become neutral under international guarantee. Chamberlain envisaged a gradual transfer of affected areas, but Hitler demanded evacuation by 1st October. The British government rejected his demand, but he remained adamant when visited by Sir Horace Wilson on 26th September.

Nevertheless, Hitler was worried by the anxiety expressed by his generals and the lack of enthusiasm for war in Germany. He wrote to Chamberlain in terms which avoided concessions, but encouraged the Prime Minister to make one more effort. Britain asked Mussolini to approach Hitler, and the Duce, thoroughly alarmed at the prospect of a general war, did so on 28th September. He prevailed on Hitler to participate in a conference to be held in Munich the following day.

From this hastily improvised meeting the Czechs, despite Anglo-French attempts to include them, were excluded. The memorandum on which agreement was based had been drawn up in the German foreign office, secretly conveyed to Rome, and produced by Mussolini as his own. It contained few significant differences from the Godesberg proposals, and was accepted on 30th September. Czechoslovakia was obliged to accept the loss of eleven thousand square miles of territory, disruption of her railway services, severe reduction of her industry and the loss of her fortifications. Eight hundred thousand Czechs became German subjects, while 250,000 Germans remained in Czechoslovakia.

Until 28th September, Hitler had been uncertain whether to gain the Sudetenland by negotiation or risk overrunning all Czechoslovakia. Mussolini's intervention decided him, but he remained determined to fulfil the boast in Operation Green.

After Munich, Czechoslovakia ceded territory to Poland and Hungary, and granted autonomy to Slovakia and Ruthenia. German influence worked to persuade the Slovaks and their

German minority to demand independence. President Hacha, Benes's successor, sought to preserve national integrity by dismissing the Slovak and Ruthenian governments in March 1939, and Hitler demonstrated his opportunism. Tiso, the deposed Slovakian Prime Minister, was invited to Berlin. He returned with a declaration of Slovakian independence, drafted in Berlin, and the threat that if it were not proclaimed Slovakia would suffer German occupation. Tiso secured a session of the Slovak Parliament and independence was declared on 14th March, an internal change which enabled Chamberlain's government to disavow its Munich guarantee of Czechoslovakia.

In any case Hitler was by then travelling to Prague. President Hacha had gone to Berlin on 14th March to plead for his country. Old, inexperienced and so ill that he fainted during talks with the Fuehrer, he was easily persuaded to telephone instructions to Prague that the German advance was not to be resisted, and two hours later troops crossed the frontier. A joint communiqué announced that Hacha had 'confidently placed the fate of the Czech people in the hands of the Fuehrer'. The Protectorate of Bohemia and Moravia was established, and soon afterwards Tiso requested similar protection in a telegram prepared for him by the German foreign office on 13th March. Hungary overran Ruthenia.

This was Hitler's last major success without recourse to war, and he had given up one of his strong cards. His previous aggressions had been veiled with appeals to the principle of national self-determination, and in Britain this justification was felt to have some force. The occupation of non-German land destroyed the illusion, and British policy, although still envisaging a general settlement without war, became firmer.

Preparations for recapturing Danzig, and territory lost to Poland in 1919, were in train before the final dismemberment of Czechoslovakia. In order to give Poland access to the sea Danzig had been separated from Germany and became a Free City where the Poles enjoyed economic privileges, while East Prussia was separated from the rest of Germany by the Polish Corridor. Much of the land regained by Poland had been lost to Prussia during the eighteenth-century partitions and was inhabited by Poles, but Poland had taken more in Silesia than she could legitimately claim.

The motive behind the Non-Aggression Pact of 1934 was to placate a suspicious neighbour until Germany was stronger. Hitler may also have contemplated securing a Polish alliance against Russia. In October 1938 Ribbentrop proposed to Lipski, the Polish ambassador, the return of Danzig, an extra-territorial road and railway across the Corridor, and a joint policy against Russia, in return for minor concessions. The Poles made it clear that they would never meet these demands, but agreed to negotiate over Danzig and improved German communications in the Corridor, a position from which they never withdrew. Meanwhile they continued to balance between Germany and Russia, convinced that if they veered too much in one direction Poland would end as a satellite. Germany's occupation of Czechoslovakia, and her successful ultimatum to Lithuania for the restoration of the Memelland shortly afterwards, increased Polish apprehension.

In March 1939 Chamberlain announced that Britain would act if Polish independence were threatened, and negotiations began for a mutual assistance pact between the two countries. This was an unexpected check for the Fuehrer, but Operation White, issued on 1st April, directed preparations to be made for an attack on Poland on 1st September. Probably Hitler expected to have achieved his ends by bluff before then, and in April denounced the Non-Aggression Pact and the Anglo-German Naval Agreement.

No further overtures were made to Warsaw. The activities of the Nazi fifth column in Danzig were stimulated and attempts made to isolate the Poles. German relations with the Balkan states were strengthened and non-aggression pacts signed with Latvia, Lithuania and Estonia. More important the Duce was finally persuaded in May to sign a military alliance, the Pact of Steel.

The most startling development was a Russo-German *rap-*

prochement. In the attempt to isolate Poland, Russia was vital. Anglo-French guarantees to Poland were of little military value without help from the Soviet Union. Neither Britain nor France was eager to approach Russia, only reluctantly did Chamberlain suggest talks, and no important British minister went to Moscow despite Stalin's invitation. This was not lost on Hitler, and the replacement of the pro-western Litvinov by Molotov, as Soviet Commissar for Foreign Affairs, gave further encouragement to Germany. Current talks for the renewal of recently expired Russo-German economic agreements became the sounding-board for wider negotiations.

Ultimately, war with Russia was inevitable while Hitler sought *Lebensraum* in the East, but it suited his immediate need to reach an agreement with her. After recent purges Stalin's army was unfit for a major war, justifiably he had little faith in the West and a deal at Poland's expense, with possible territorial gains accruing in eastern Europe, was inviting.

Both sides were wary, but a personal exchange of notes between Hitler and Stalin cleared the way for the Nazi-Soviet Pact of 24th August 1939. Publicly it was a non-aggression pact, but secret protocols recognized Finland, Estonia and Latvia as Russian spheres of interest and Lithuania and Vilna as German. A partition of Poland was envisaged and Russia's economic interest recognized in the Rumanian province of Bessarabia.

Hitler seems to have expected that news of the Pact would detach Britain and France from Poland, but in this he was mistaken and made a final attempt to complete Polish isolation. His approaches resulted in Sir Nevile Henderson, the British ambassador in Berlin, bringing a Polish offer to negotiate. Immediately Hitler insisted that a plenipotentiary with full powers to reach immediate agreement should be sent, but the British government declined to urge this upon Warsaw. On the 30th August Hitler published, for the first time, a complete list of his demands on Poland, partly in an attempt to convince the Germans that he was seeking to preserve peace, but also to persuade London to put further pressure on Poland. Under Anglo-French pressure

Warsaw instructed Lipski to talk to Ribbentrop, but the German government had already broken the diplomatic cipher, and knew that Lipski could not reach immediate agreement, so that his interview at the Wilhelmstrasse was futile.

Meanwhile Alfred Naujocks, one of Heydrich's men, had been waiting, since 10th August, near the Polish frontier to fake a Polish attack on the German radio station at Gleiwitz. He was supposed to stage an attack, broadcast a short statement indicating that Gleiwitz had been seized by Poles, and then retire. Material evidence was to take the form of a number of criminals, killed by lethal injections and peppered with gunshot wounds, whose corpses were to be left lying near the station dressed in Polish uniforms. In the event Naujocks seems to have used only one body. Otherwise this clumsy episode was carried out according to plan and used as evidence of Polish infringement of German territory. At dawn on 1st September 1939, the German Panzers swept into Poland. Hitler had finally risked the use of naked force and plunged the Third Reich into the war which would destroy it.

Hitler still hoped that Britain and France would remain neutral, but on 3rd September, after Mussolini's abortive attempt to arrange a second 'Munich', they declared war. They gave their ally little assistance and by the end of September Polish resistance was over. The speed of the German *blitzkrieg* had surprised the world and seriously worried Stalin, who prepared to occupy those regions allotted to him in the August Pact. He also used Hitler's need for a free hand in the West to secure alterations to the original. Lithuania became part of the Russian sphere and Poland was partitioned. Western Poland returned to the Reich and central Poland was occupied as the General-Government. Hitler had made considerable sacrifices, including the Baltic States, traditional German outposts, and much of Poland including the oil region of Borislav-Drohobycz. The Suwalki Triangle on the East Prussian border was his only territorial gain, but he was free to turn West.

Hitler had determined on Operation Yellow, against the West, by the end of September. In the ensuing months of the 'phoney war' he planned, and destroyed the not very forceful opposition of his generals. Bad weather caused postponement from November to January, when the capture of a German staff officer who crashed in Belgium carrying full operational plans necessitated a further delay.

By this time Hitler was becoming attracted to Admiral Raeder's scheme for attacking Norway, which he advocated on the grounds of securing bases for action against British shipping, and securing winter communications with Sweden, whence came much of Germany's iron ore. Through Rosenberg, Raeder found a highly placed Norwegian collaborator, Vikdun Quisling, but the German invasion force was eventually made so large that collaboration was unimportant. The British and Norwegian governments were slow to guard against the attack, which was launched, simultaneously with one on Denmark, on 9th April. By the end of the month success was assured, and on 10th May the Fuehrer unleashed Operation Yellow. The German armies raced across France and the Low Countries. Their only failure was to prevent the evacuation of 330,000 British and French soldiers from Dunkirk between 27th May and 4th June, due to a tactical error for which Hitler was responsible. An area of southern France, called Vichy France, retained certain rights of self-government under Nazi tutelage until 1942, while the remainder of France and the Low Countries became occupied territory.

On 22nd June 1941, exactly one year after the French Armistice, Hitler invaded Russia. During the intervening twelve months he had pursued three lines of policy. Attempts were made to defeat Britain, the Balkans were overrun, and preparations made for Operation Barbarossa, the attack on Russia. To some extent they overlapped, but may be dealt with more conveniently as separate items.

Until June 1940 Hitler had never seriously considered the invasion of Britain. He was convinced that, after the fall of France, Britain would come to terms, since all he wanted was a free hand in Europe. When his assumption proved false he became inter-

E

ested in Raeder's invasion scheme, but neither the *Luftwaffe* nor the German Navy was able to create the necessary conditions and in practice Operation Sea-Lion ended in October 1940. Heavy bombing raids on Britain continued. Attempts were made to secure the entry of Spain and Vichy France into the war to harass Britain's Mediterranean bases, and Operation Felix was drawn up for an attack on Gibraltar, but all these schemes failed. In September 1940, Mussolini attacked Egypt but, after the battle of Sidi Barrani, his armies were in headlong flight by December. During spring, 1941, unsuccessful attempts were made to persuade Japan to attack Singapore.

At the end of March Rommel's *Afrika Korps* was despatched to help the Italians and by the end of April the Germans were back on the Egyptian border. Meanwhile the German occupation of Greece had dislodged British forces from Crete and Britain's middle-eastern situation, as Churchill and Wavell acknowledged, was serious. Raeder and Rommel asked for a major offensive, but the Fuehrer would not agree. He was determined to deal first with Russia.

Fulfilment of the plans for attacking Russia was delayed by the Balkan situation, which had to be dealt with as an incidental complication. Russia had occupied territory due to her under the agreement with Germany, and during 1940 made further demands on Rumania. It became essential to check Russian expansion westward, while 'Barbarossa' matured, and to stabilize the Balkan situation generally, since Bulgaria and Hungary both had revisionist claims on Rumania. German intervention settled these and in September 1940 King Carol of Rumania abdicated, leaving power in the hands of General Antonescu, who so admired Hitler that Rumania became a German satellite.

Unfortunately for the Fuehrer, Mussolini disturbed the equilibrium by attacking Greece, despite Hitler's warnings that he should not. The reluctance of Bulgaria, Yugoslavia and Turkey to join the Axis had been strengthened, Russian suspicions about the Balkans aroused, and Britain given the opportunity to secure bases in Greece. Therefore Germany was obliged to intervene, particularly in view of Mussolini's inability to defeat Greece on his own.

In order to secure free passage for German troops to Greece, the agreements of Hungary, Rumania, Bulgaria and Yugoslavia were necessary. These had been obtained by the 25th March, but on the night of 26–27th March a group of Yugoslav officers carried out a *coup d'état* against their government's policy. Hitler was furious. Ten days later improvised plans were put into operation and simultaneous attacks launched on Yugoslavia and Greece. By the end of the month both were defeated. Greece was occupied but Yugoslavia was wiped out of existence, divided between Germany, her Balkan allies and Italy.

During the whole of this time plans for the invasion of Russia had been implemented. These preparations had been carefully concealed from Hitler's allies and attempts made to divert Japanese activity into the Pacific. The Fuehrer had no intention of sharing German *Lebensraum*. To allay Russian suspicions, further trade agreements were made and every effort made to fulfil German deliveries of machinery even when it could usefully have been employed in the war effort. On the Russian side, Stalin continued to try to buy time by making huge deliveries of grain which only whetted the German appetite and revived in Hitler's mind the ideas expressed in Chapter 26 of *Mein Kampf.*

On 22nd June 1941 Russia was invaded and German armies penetrated deeply into the Soviet Union, but the successful *blitzkrieg* the Fuehrer had expected proved unattainable, and with the onset of winter Hitler's generals, at least, could foresee a repetition of the disasters which had once overtaken Charles XII of Sweden and Napoleon. On 6th December the Red Armies mounted an offensive along the whole Central Russian Front, and the threat to Moscow was averted.

By now Hitler's judgment was leading him down the road to disaster, and five days later he declared war on America in support of Japan. On 7th December the Japanese attacked the American naval base at Pearl Harbour. Hitler knew that Japanese relations with America were deteriorating but was surprised by a manoeuvre so much in his own style. He unfeignedly admired what the Japanese had done although his reaction might well have been different. He had tried to persuade Japan to attack Singapore to harass Britain and to dissuade America from entering the war, and recently Ribbentrop had urged Japan to attack Russia from the East. Hitler had never advocated a Japanese attack on America, but when it took place he rapidly decided to support his ally, and never appears to have considered the wisdom of deferring such an engagement until Russia had been defeated.

The first reason for his misjudgment was that he regarded war with the U.S.A. as inevitable sooner or later. Indeed the current American assistance to Britain amounted to a state of war in his eyes, and twice in October 1941 U-boats had engaged American destroyers, so that a declaration of war simply clarified the situation. Furthermore, he grossly misunderstood the nature of American society and never perceived her significance as a world power. A racially mixed non-authoritarian people must, he assumed, be decadent, and Pearl Harbour was taken to illustrate his assumption. Like the German High Command in 1917, he overlooked the possibility of American intervention in Europe on the massive scale of 1944.

By the end of 1941 Hitler was engaged in a war which he could not hope to win, but before it was lost the Nazis used the short time left to them in trying to establish their New Order in occupied Europe.

CHAPTER NINE

Nazism's New European Order

FORTY miles north of Hanover, set in desolate heathland, are the relics of Belsen camp. Overgrown mounds bear notices recording the several hundred anonymous dead buried beneath each one, and close by stand a number of memorials. One, erected by the British, commemorates with restraint 'those who died in this place', while the Jewish stone remembers those who died at the hands of the 'murderous Nazis'. Such is the archaeology of the New European Order.

Although Hitler often referred to it in his writings and speeches, the New Order was never the subject of any detailed, overall plan. Nevertheless there is ample evidence, in the speeches of Nazi leaders, and in the decrees issued for the government of occupied territories, to make its purpose clear. The New Europe would be economically exploited for the benefit of the *Herren-volk*, the master race. This Aryan caste might incorporate suitable elements from conquered populations, but the *untermen-schen* sub-humans, like Jews, Slavs, Polish intellectuals and Soviet Commissars, were to be exterminated or employed as slave labour.

To certain of the staff in his Economic Department Goering gave the instruction: 'Whenever you come across anything that may be needed by the German people you must be after it like a bloodhound. It must be taken out . . . and brought to Germany.'

In the notorious speech to an audience of his S.S. officers at Posen, in 1943, Himmler declared: 'What the nations can offer in the way of good blood of our type, we will take, if necessary

by kidnapping their children and raising them here with us.' The
Reichsfuehrer S.S. went on to express his indifference to the fate
of 10,000 Russian women digging a German anti-tank ditch, so
long as it was finished, while, in 1942, Martin Bormann, Hitler's
deputy, wrote to Rosenberg in the following terms: 'The Slavs
are to work for us. In so far as we don't need them, they may die.
Therefore compulsory vaccination and German health services
are superfluous. The fertility of the Slavs is undesirable. . . .
Education is dangerous. . . . Religion we leave to them as a
means of diversion. As for food they won't get any more than is
absolutely necessary. We are the masters. We come first.'

None of this was rabble-rousing demagogy. The Nazi leaders
meant precisely what they said on these occasions. The reign of
terror, plunder and extermination, which sprang from their nightmare vision, is unparalleled in European history, and differed in
kind from many other gross inhumanities inflicted by men on
their fellows. The early industrialization of Great Britain caused
considerable human sufferings, but the maltreatment of child
workers was not its ultimate purpose, and materially its long-
term benefits have been of immense value. Nazism brought no
long-term benefits, and terror and extermination became, in the
hands of many of its agents, ends in themselves.

No attempt will be made here to relate the history of each
country under German occupation, but only to indicate some of
the outstanding features of Nazi policy wherever it operated. In
general its administration was most confused, and its methods
most brutal, in the East, but in Western Europe it was far from
benevolent.

The government of occupied Europe further illustrates the
inefficiency of Nazi dictatorship. Hitler became increasingly
absorbed in the conduct of the war and, until November 1944,
spent most of his time at his permanent headquarters at Wolfs-
schanze, in the gloomy forests of East Prussia. Civil administrators
were left to flounder in the usual Nazi welter of personal rivalries
and conflicting spheres of authority.

Alfred Rosenberg was Minister for the Eastern Territories

including the *Ostland* (Latvia, Lithuania, Estonia and White Russia), and the Ukraine. Each was ruled by a *Reichskommissar* below whom were *Generalkommissars* and *Gebeitskommissars*, intended as a chain of command, but forming, rather, a series of conflicting authorities. Erich Koch, *Reichskommissar* of the Ukraine spent most of his time in his *Gau* of East Prussia, and was in perpetual conflict with Rosenberg, his nominal chief. Both men compiled dossiers of complaint against each other, which they forwarded to Hitler, who did nothing to resolve their differences.

The quality of many officials in occupied territory was questionable; the *Gebeitskommissar* of Slonim in White Russia was a criminal sadist, and Hans Frank remained Governor-General of unincorporated Poland, after his fall from grace, simply because his was a thankless job.

The extent to which native populations might retain some share in government remained a controversial issue. Puppet administrations survived in Norway, Holland and Czechoslovakia, but with no power. Autonomy for the Ukraine had its supporters, and each of the three former Baltic states had a National Directorate, which prolonged its formal existence by fleeing to Germany even after the Russians reoccupied its homeland.

Confusion was aggravated by the independent activities of the S.S. and S.D., and in occupied Russia, Goering's Office of the Four Year Plan enjoyed an independent monopoly of economic exploitation, while rear-area commanders of the *Wehrmacht*, concerned to keep supply-lines open, and check partisan warfare, acted without reference to anyone else. The *Reichsbahn*, the German railway authority, took over the railways and was responsible to no one but itself, and Fritz Sauckel's labour commissioners conducted their slave-raiding activities irrespective of labour requirements in the countries they visited. The bureaucratic chaos was such that Hans Frank found that 40,000 German civil servants were too few to govern territory 'half the size of Italy'.

Terror was the basic instrument of Nazi government. Shortly

before the invasion of Poland Hitler spoke in terms of proceeding
'. . . against the Poles after the end of the campaign with relent-
less vigour', and of the extermination of the Polish intelligentsia.

In the case of Russia the notorious Commissar and Jurisdiction
Decrees were issued in May and June 1941, based on instructions
given by Hitler to his generals in March, three months before
'Barbarossa' was launched. Walter Warlimont, head of the
National Defence Office, drafted the decree making anyone,
identified as a political functionary, liable to summary execution.
At Rosenberg's suggestion, those who offered no resistance might
be spared, but no clear definition of a Commissar was ever given,
and the S.D. enjoyed *carte blanche* in selecting their victims. The
second decree, drafted by Rudolf Lehmann, the High Command's
legal expert, provided that any civilian suspect might be shot
without trial, at the discretion of any officer of rank equivalent
to battalion commander or above, while there was no obligation
upon the Army to proceed against its own men for offences
against civilians.

After the war a number of generals asserted that the decrees had
outraged them. They gave specious reasons why they had not
refused point-blank to sanction their operation, including the
alleged belief that, under conditions of active service far from
Berlin, they could be circumvented. In fact they were vigorously
employed, but two examples of their horror will suffice. In
September 1941 Professor Kanaiev was shot because, as secretary
of the Literary Institute of the Academy of Science, he was classed
as a Commissar. An old man, he was captured while in charge
of a mobile cinema, which had been showing to a railway protection battalion of over-age reservists. Under the Jurisdiction
Decree peasant women and their children, who attempted to feed
prisoners being marched to rear areas, were shot without
question.

During the struggle against Russian partisans, methods became
even more ferocious. The notorious Dierlewanger S.S. Regiment
specialized in marching women and children across the minefields protecting partisan hideouts. In pacified partisan areas,

surviving inhabitants were supposed to be moved to camps, prior to transportation to Germany for forced labour, but often they were shot instead. In 'Operation Cottbus', launched, in 1942, against the partisan 'Republic of Lake Pelik', 15,000 people were killed. Of these, 5000 were only 'suspects', and 4000 died 'spotting mines'. Captured weapons totalled 1100 rifles and 326 small arms, an indication of how many of the 'partisans' had offered active resistance.

In the West, the bizarre *Nacht und Nebel Erlass*, the Night and Fog Decree, was an instrument of tyranny. Issued personally by Hitler in December 1941, it ordered the arrest of persons endangering security. They were to be taken away into the unknown of Germany, and no information, even of their burial place, was to be given to their relatives.

The shooting of hostages was a common form of reprisal, often in the ratio of one hundred for every German killed by resistance forces, and in France 29,660 hostages were executed during the war. In Denmark a system flourished whereby well-known personalities were murdered, and their bodies left lying in the road, or elsewhere, as a dire warning to those who opposed German rule.

The atmosphere of occupied Western Europe was evoked in the evidence, given at the Nuremberg Trials, by Professor van der Essen, of Louvain University. He described an actual, but typical, day in occupied Belgium. An early morning knock on the door was immediately—though incorrectly—assumed to be the Gestapo. Later, the postman passed on a warning that van der Essen's son, a former soldier, was to be arrested, and he was sent into hiding. On several occasions during the day, the trams, on which the professor travelled, were stopped, and their passengers searched, in routine checks. One village he passed through between Brussels and Louvain had just had some of its inhabitants taken as hostages, while at the university he learned that a number of his colleagues had been arrested the day before, disappearing into Night and Fog.

The razing of villages, sometimes with the execution of the

whole population, was not unknown. It occurred in Russia, Poland, Greece, Yugoslavia, Czechoslovakia, France and Norway, but the most infamous cases were those of Lidice and Oradour-sur-Glâne.

On 29th May 1942, two Czechs, Jan Kubic and Josef Gabeik, hurled a bomb at the Mercedes sports car driven by Reinhard Heydrich, and on 4th June he died from his injuries. As Acting Protector of Bohemia and Moravia, Heydrich had become so convinced of his popularity with his subjects that he dispensed with the motorcade of security agents who usually accompanied the Nazi leaders. It was his undoing. In the hecatomb that followed, hundreds of Czechs were killed, but the destruction of Lidice was outstanding in its savagery. All the men over sixteen were executed, and several women. Most of the women were sent to Ravensbrueck. The children were dispersed to orphanages and camps. Every building was burned, the ruins dynamited and the site levelled.

In June 1944, exactly two years after Lidice, a detachment of the S.S. division, Das Reich, surrounded the French village of Oradour-sur-Glâne. The inhabitants were herded into barns and the church. The buildings were fired, and those who tried to escape shot. Of the 652 inhabitants only ten survived.

The treatment of prisoners of war, particularly Russians, was intentionally brutal, and nearly four million Soviet troops died in captivity. The Commissar Decree provided that Jews and Commissars should be sorted out and executed. Admiral Canaris made a half-hearted attempt to obtain clear screening rules, but nothing was done, except that executions took place outside the camp, and *stalag* commanders were relieved of responsibility for screening. The S.D. were only too eager to perform both tasks, although troops as well as security police were employed in firing squads.

Rules for the treatment of prisoners were drawn up by Lieutenant-General Hermann Reinecke, the Army's chief of P.O.W. affairs; they emphasized the use of clubs, whips and firearms in maintaining discipline. The Commissar Order and the Reinecke rules were not in themselves sufficient to account for nearly four million deaths, and there were other causes of such loss of life.

The first lay in the great encirclement battles fought at the beginning of the Russian campaign. Huge Russian armies were cut off and surrounded, 655,000 at Kiev, and 663,000 at Viasma, for example. These men had often been starving for days before they surrendered. The Germans had no food or medical supplies for them, and many were quite unable to stand long marches to rear areas.

In addition, between July and November 1941, an order existed forbidding the evacuation of Russian prisoners to Germany, although camps were available for them, lest they should spread Marxism among their guards and the civilian population. Thus many were kept for months in rear-area and transit camps. At the Uman brickworks, men lay in the open because the huts were choked with excrement, and fought each other for occasional bowls of soup, and at Stalino the death-rate was 80 per cent a year by December 1941. In one lecture theatre of the requisitioned High School, there was no space to sit, and in another lay heaps of the dead and dying, according to Major Herre who visited the place.

The final cause of death was the policy of Herbert Bache, Director of the Food Ministry. His instructions were responsible for the death of half a million Russian prisoners between November 1941 and February 1942, when fewer prisoners were being taken and it would have been easy to organize food and accommodation. The original scale of rations for Russian prisoners amounted to half a pound of bread a day, about one pound of meat and one of fat each month, and a pound and a half of sugar. In practice this meant thin soup and bread. Most of the bread was made from rye bran, cellulose, sugar beet, straw and leaves, and the meat taken from animals which had not passed through the slaughterhouse.

Western prisoners, particularly the American and British, were better treated in general. Such cases as the murder of eighty-three Americans at Malmedy in 1944, or the shooting of a hundred men of the Royal Norfolks at Le Paradis farm in Belgium in 1940, were due to acts of individual cruelty, although those responsible were not punished. Captured aircrews received more severe treatment. Civilians were encouraged to lynch airmen who bailed out, and Hitler himself ordered the execution of fifty R.A.F. men who escaped from captivity in 1944. In the same year forty-seven British, American and Dutch Air Force officers were murdered at Mauthausen Concentration Camp by being forced to carry increasingly heavy loads of stone up the steps of a quarry. From October 1942 onwards captured commando units, even those in uniform, were shot.

Both civilians and prisoners of war were employed on forced labour, in direct contradiction, in the case of the latter, to international agreements. By the autumn of 1944 seven and a half million foreign civilians were at work in Germany. Some were volunteers, but the majority were conscripts, housed in concentration camps, or labour camps which were little better. Various departments shared in organizing the slave trade of the Third Reich. Albert Speer, Minister for Armament and War Production, was primarily responsible for deciding the numbers required; Fritz Sauckel, Plenipotentiary for Labour, was responsible for recruitment; Herbert Bache determined their rations, and the *Reichsbahn* provided the appalling rolling stock which carried them to Germany. The S.D. and Gestapo were their only judicial authority. The activity of Sauckel's agents brought complaints from German officials in Russia that economic exploitation was being made more difficult and partisan warfare aggravated, but this remained another inter-departmental feud, which Hitler failed to settle.

Satisfying Speer's demands for labour, for example two million souls in the last four months of 1942, necessitated the use of ruthless methods. Some volunteers, often skilled, were eager to escape from Russia, but church congregations and cinema audiences were arrested *en masse*. In Western Europe, sections of a town were sealed off and all the able-bodied inside deported; in the East, villages were razed and the population forcibly recruited. Travelling conditions were murderous, and Sauckel's request for uncrowded carriages, heating, water, and feeding, ignored by the *Reichsbahn*. Otto Braeutigam, of Rosenberg's staff, organized a relief agency for Eastern workers, which reported that in the six months prior to September 1942, 5 per cent habitually arrived unfit for work, and had to be sent back. In one returning train several dead were found in locked box-cars, venereal and T.B. cases lay together on straw, and women had flung their dead children out of the windows.

Living conditions, regulated by a Himmler order of February 1942, were only marginally better. Eastern workers wore a badge to enable Aryans to avoid racial contamination, and their camps were surrounded by barbed-wire and heavily guarded. Later, slight improvements were made. Workers were given two or three hours' free time each week, although they could not use public transport, eating-houses or entertainment, and eventually the barbed-wire was removed, maternity wards provided, and even books and entertainment in some cases. The improvements were probably due to Goebbels's intervention with Hitler, when a new drive for Eastern labour was begun in 1943, and the scale of any potential slave rebellion was much increased.

The worst evils of slave labour were probably due to Himmler's desire to obtain some of its profit for the S.S. Before the war, he had begun schemes to employ the inmates of Sachsenhausen, Dachau and Buchenwald in quarrying sand and gravel, and manufacturing bricks and cement, in order to participate in Speer's grandiose plans for rebuilding Berlin and Nuremberg. To this end he formed DEST and DAW, two commercial companies, run by the *Verwaltungsamt*, the business management office of the S.S. under Oswald Pohl. Heydrich and the camp inspectorate disliked these schemes, being interested only in extermination, so that it remained usual to maltreat and starve those performing useful work. Surviving camp rosters show that few inmates were usefully employed, and at Sachsenhausen one commandant used his charges to build a yacht for him.

By February 1942 the Russian campaign had caused an arma-

ments crisis, and Speer was moved to protest at the waste of
concentration camp labour. Himmler, believing that, if he could
make all the necessary equipment, Hitler would allow him to
expand the *Waffen S.S.*, asked to be allowed to use camp labour
to make munitions. Under Speer's influence, Hitler followed his
own inclination and refused, but Speer offered a compromise,
under which Himmler should supply camp labour to civilian
armaments firms, and receive a proportion of their output.

In order to achieve his own ends, under this arrangement,
Himmler clearly needed to expand the camp population. He
reached a secret agreement with Thierack, the Minister of Justice,
under which Eastern workers could be deported to concentration
camps for the crime of being 'asocial'. 'Working to death' was
specifically mentioned as the fate of these unfortunates, thousands
of whom found themselves incarcerated under the simplified
procedure. By 1944 Speer was complaining that his labour force
was being stolen at a rate of between 30,000 and 40,000 a month,
and eventually Himmler had to agree to release short term
offenders when their sentence expired.

Speer's anxiety was solely due to the enfeebled condition of
camp labourers, which made them useless. They were leased to
industrialists, so weak that many died at their work. There seems
to have been neither scruple against using them, nor competition
for their services. I.G. Farben gave them a daily bowl of soup,
Krupps nothing. The Hungarian Jewesses, working for them at
the end of the war, existed in unspeakable conditions. Covered
with open wounds and sores, they were riddled with diseases,
and wore only a piece of sacking and no shoes. Their barracks
were infested with vermin, and their food wholly inadequate.
Western workers were often better treated, but in the Krupps
factory at Essen Frenchmen were housed in fives, in dog kennels
three feet high, nine long and six wide. Yet the worst exploiters
of slave labour were probably small firms who ran requisitioned
Polish factories. Walter Toebbens controlled a number of these,
and took labour from the Warsaw ghetto. When it was to be
liquidated he lured his workers into S.S. labour camps with

promises of protection and, until they were slaughtered, shared his profits with the S.S. police leader, Odilo Globocnik.

Many imported labourers worked on farms, where conditions were often tolerable despite bureaucratic attempts to make them otherwise. There were also schemes to bring women to Germany as domestic workers. One such derived from the Fuehrer himself, who seems to have admired Ukranian women for their chastity and Nordic appearance. Hence in 1942 he decided that half a million Ukranian girls should be allowed to come voluntarily to Germany to work as domestic servants and enjoy the privilege of being germanized. In fact no more than 15,000 ever volunteered.

Child labour was often conscripted, sometimes with the racial purposes of destroying enemy biological potential and finding candidates for germanization. Action Hay, which originated with the Army, entailed the deportation of over 40,000 Russian children; Sauckel's officials took anyone over the age of ten, and Himmler once produced a half-baked scheme for employing children to pick the *Kok Sagys*, the Russian rubber-producing dandelion.

To the very end the German attitude to conscripted workers, at least from the East, was bedevilled by three characteristics. First there was the apparent fear that every bewildered White Russian or Ukrainian, speaking no German, was ready at the first opportunity to spread the gospel of Marxism. In addition they acted under the impression that the Slavs were sub-humans who responded only to brutal ill-treatment. That many of them had no love for Stalin's Russia, and would have worked willingly enough under tolerable conditions, never seems to have penetrated the N.C.O. mentality of their overseers. Finally, there was the desire—seen at its worst in Himmler's schemes—to get something for nothing, and the refusal to face the fact of industrial life that ill-paid, half-starved labour, given no incentive, is grossly underproductive.

The total plunder taken from occupied Europe will never be accurately assessed. In money alone the amount was astronomical. The gold and foreign holdings of national banks were seized, and 'credits', 'fines' and 'occupation costs' demanded. By the end of the war it has been estimated that France had paid sixty billion marks, and Belgium and the Netherlands, two-thirds of their national incomes.

Requisitions in kind were even more severe. From France, it is estimated, were taken nine million tons of cereals and 74 per cent of her steel, among other items. Ruthless exploitation of Russian territory was planned well before the invasion, and indeed one motive for attacking the Ukraine was to acquire its grain resources. The huge amounts of wheat which had been sent to Germany under recent Russo-German trade agreements acted as a stimulus for conquest. The Germans calculated the value of deliveries from Russia at four billion marks, and, ironically, it has been shown that they could probably have obtained more from normal trade. Partisan warfare, labour conscription, mass murder and bureaucratic inefficiency all reduced the industrial and agricultural potential of occupied Eastern Europe. Art treasures were looted, particularly from France, on an enormous scale, probably to satisfy the avarice of Goering and Hitler more than for any other reason.

All that has been considered so far was tyrannical, but not essentially Nazi. Secret police, maltreatment of prisoners and forced labour have occurred in many parts of the world. The remaining aspects of the New Order were essentially Nazi, and refute any suggestion that Nazi theory had no application in practice.

Himmler was always eager to extend his authority into as many fields as possible, but his one unchallenged kingdom consisted of the concentration camps, and he constantly sought ways of using his hapless subjects. Forced labour was one, and so-called scientific and medical research was another. It has been argued that the experiments carried out on concentration camp inmates were the result of sheer sadism, but in general this was probably not true. Himmler and the doctors with whom he co-operated were mad. They believed without question in the racial nonsense of

Nazi propaganda. To conduct experiments on *untermenschen* for the increase of scientific knowledge was no different from experimenting on mice or guinea-pigs. It is true that no increase in knowledge resulted, but this is not evidence that sadism was the original motive for experiment.

In 1941 Professor Hirt of the University of Strasbourg expressed to Rudolf Brandt, Himmler's adjutant, his desire to add the skulls of Jewish-Bolshevik Commissars to the anatomical collection of his University Institute. This was an interest close to Himmler's heart, and he directed Wolfram Sievers to assist Hirt. Sievers ran the S.S. Institute for Research into Heredity, and he assembled 115 people at Auschwitz for 'anthropological measurement'. They were then transferred to Natzweiler camp, gassed, and their bodies given to Hirt, who conducted a series of meaningless anthropological studies on the corpses and skeletons, which continued almost until the Allies reached Strasbourg in 1944.

Dr. Sigmund Rascher appears to have been the initiator of a number of experiments supposedly for the benefit of German aircrews. He had earned Himmler's good opinions when his wife, an acquaintance of Frau Himmler, had borne three children when over the age of forty-eight. Worship of Aryan motherhood was an item of Himmler's folklore, and Dr. Rascher enjoyed reflected glory. While on a Luftwaffe medical course in 1941, he asked Himmler to provide him with human beings for investigation into the effects of high-altitude flying. A Luftwaffe decompression chamber was erected at Dachau, and air pumped out to simulate high altitudes, while the effects on the unfortunates inside were recorded. Some two hundred prisoners were used, of whom about eighty died, while the remainder were afterwards executed. Rascher later conducted experiments to discover how much cold a human being could endure, and how best to re-warm someone who had survived extreme cold. Experiments of the first kind consisted of immersing subjects in cold water until they died. Various means of re-warming were tried, including the use of 'animal heat'. Oswald Pohl provided four prostitutes from Ravensbrueck, and incurred a reprimand from Himmler, since at least one of them was German. Rascher continued his labours until 1944, when it was discovered that his three children had in fact been kidnapped from orphanages. This treachery to German motherhood so outraged Himmler that the Raschers were incarcerated in Dachau and Ravensbrueck, from which they never emerged.

Between 1942 and 1944 a positive orgy of experiment occurred in various camps. At Ravensbrueck, Polish girls were inflicted with gas-gangrened wounds by Karl Gebhardt, a lifelong friend of Himmler. Professor Mugrowski studied the effects of poisoned bullets. At Buchenwald victims were infected with typhus, while there and at Dachau gipsies were made to live on sea water. Sterilization experiments were carried out on Jewesses at Auschwitz and Ravensbrueck.

Closely associated with the idea of *Lebensraum* and the strengthening of the master-race was the repatriation of all racial Germans to the Fatherland. To Himmler, nothing could have been more natural, and in October 1939 he was appointed head of the R.K.F.D.V., the Reich Commissarist for the Strengthening of German Nationhood. It was decreed that in Poland Germany had achieved part of her *Lebensraum*. Himmler was to bring back eligible racial Germans, weed out foreigners, and with the new subjects and space create German colonies.

The R.K.F.D.V. was to co-ordinate the work of the police in Poland with two S.S. offices, V.O.M.I. and R.U.S.H.A. The former had originally been attached to the party office and concerned with the welfare of Germans abroad. It ended as a press-gang which conscripted any German-looking individual in occupied territory into the *Waffen* S.S. R.U.S.H.A. was the S.S. marriage-bureau, but it came to be involved in kidnapping children suitable for germanization, deporting slave labour to Germany and undesirables from resettlement areas, and deciding who should be executed for miscegenation with Germans.

The activities of the R.K.F.D.V. flourished during the 'phoney war'. Undesirables were expelled from annexed Poland and racial Germans brought in from the Baltic States, Volhynia, Bessarabia,

Bukovina, Bosnia and the Dobrudja. Many of these could not be absorbed, and 100,000 were still living in camps in Western Poland in the summer of 1943. Under the threat of partisan warfare 36,000 were restored to Lithuania, and placed in farms along the communication roads between East Prussia and Latvia in order to protect them. Elsewhere little repatriation was done, and German officials waxed fat while native Germans became cannon-fodder or misplaced persons. Various colonization projects were drafted—to move the South Tyrolese to the Crimea, and the Dutch to Latvia—but little came of them, and after 1942 nothing further was heard of colonization schemes.

Hitler had no idealism about a united Europe, except as Germany's economic expansion ground, but Himmler was full of it. The idea of a European S.S. may have occurred to him when the Nordic lands of Scandinavia were overrun, and he found an equally woolly-minded enthusiast in Gottlob Berger, Chief of Staff of the *Waffen S.S.*

At first the foreign units were never above battalion strength, but after 1944 Himmler was head of the Replacement Army and Hitler had come to accept his arguments that foreign S.S. units reduced the potential strength of resistance movements. Thus France provided the Charlemagne division, Holland the Nederland, Belgium the Wallonia and Flanders, and Scandinavia the Nordland. In the Russian campaigns their field record was unequalled, and after the liberation of France they became fanatics since surrender meant, for them, execution as collaborators. The units raised in Eastern Europe were unwilling, conscripted racial Germans, and some units were in fact wholly Slav. Their morale was of the lowest and not even Gottlob Berger could pretend that they represented the New Order.

Most infamous among the catalogue of Nazi atrocities is the attempt to exterminate European Jewry. The Final Solution of the Jewish problem was the ultimate expression of the anti-semitism in *Mein Kampf*, and the logical conclusion of a process which began with the Nuremberg Laws.

The number of Jews slaughtered in Europe was estimated by

the World Jewish Congress, and at the Nuremberg Trials, at a figure approaching six millions. Gerald Reitlinger, in his exhaustive study of the Final Solution, reached a lower figure of approximately four and a half millions. Since there were some ten million Jews living, in 1939, in territory overrun by the Germans, it is reasonable to accept that about half that number was killed. The difference between the two estimates mentioned is due largely to lack of information about the death of Jews in territory now controlled by Soviet Russia. In the most important sense the precise number is irrelevant. Mr. Reitlinger has put it: '. . . that it does not make the guilt of the living German any less, if the figure of six millions turns out to be an over-estimate. . . . Whether six millions died, or five millions, or less, it was still the most systematic extermination of a race in human history. Moreover, once the principle of the murders is proved, there is no particular magic in additional millions.'

Even before the war a beginning had been made in the deportation of Jews from the Reich into Poland. Many were simply dumped across the Silesian frontier in open fields, and only the action of an international relief agency mitigated their circumstances.

In 1939 there began deportations into the General Government of Poland, and the concentration of Jews in ghettos, at Warsaw and elsewhere, and labour camps. The Germans controlled the ghettoes here, as in other countries where they were established, through a Jewish Council. Various forms of economic pressure steadily increased the hardship of ghetto life, so that hundreds died in them before the extermination camps began to function.

With the invasion of Russia the murderous activities of the *Einsatzgruppen*, or Action Groups, began. These had first been organized in Poland, by Heydrich, to round up Jews and place them in ghettos. At the beginning of the Russian campaign four such groups were formed for the purpose of carrying out extermination. Otto Ohlendorf, the leader of *Einsatzgruppe* D, testified at Nuremberg as to the methods used. The prominent Jews of a village or town were obliged to provide a list of those

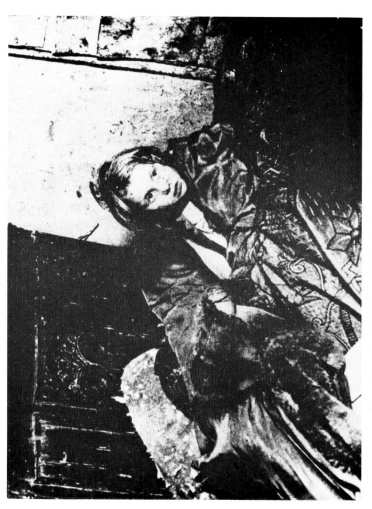

PLATE IV. This child, in a Polish ghetto, was just one of the anonymous victims of the New Order.

of their race, in preparation for 're-settlement'. The victims were transported to a prepared execution ground, consisting of a deep ditch, shot, and their bodies buried in the ditch. Over 30,000 Jews were massacred in similar fashion on 29th and 30th September 1941 at Kiev. Altogether the *Einsatzgruppen* were probably responsible for the murder of about 700,000 Jews.

It was after the beginning of the Russian campaign, at some time in the summer or autumn of 1941, that the Fuehrer Order on the Final Solution—which was never put on paper—was transmitted from Hitler, through Goering, to Heydrich, who held an inter-ministry conference on the subject at Gross Wannsee in January 1942. He explained that European Jewry was to be brought to the East and worked to death. Those who survived would be put to death. Broadly speaking this was done, since at the *Vernichtungslager*, extermination camps, which were opened, incoming trainloads were divided into those fit for work and those for immediate execution, although those fit for work seldom survived more than a few weeks and did little productive work.

The origin of the *Vernichtungslager* is to some extent obscure, but it was in part a direct continuation of the work of those responsible for the pre-war euthanasia programme. Himmler's orderly mind disliked the random activities of the *Einsatzgruppen*, which were not easily concealed, and he almost fainted at the sight of an execution held for his benefit at Minsk in 1941. It was soon after this episode that Christian Wirth, who worked on the euthanasia programme, was employed adapting lorries as gassing vehicles, which were used by the *Einsatzgruppen* by September 1941. By the end of the year Wirth and a chemical expert, Dr. Kallmeyer, working under the general instructions of Adolf Eichmann, had established gassing vans in a disused chateau, known as Chelmno, near the Lodz ghetto. The first death camp was in existence.

Between March and July 1942 three more camps were opened at Belsec, Sobibor and Treblinka. In these four camps over two million Jews were murdered in the next eighteen months, in the course of 'Action Reinhard', fittingly named in tribute to the memory of Heydrich. Carbon monoxide was pumped into the gas chambers by dismounted diesel engines, and the hideous work of removing corpses stained with blood and excreta, and burying them, was carried out by the *sonderkommando*, groups of able-bodied Jewish slaves. Any property the victims still possessed, down to their spectacles and the gold fillings in their teeth, was appropriated by the S.S.

In the autumn of 1943 the death camp machinery had already swallowed up Jews from Germany, Austria, the Balkans and Western Europe. By the summer of 1942 scores of trainloads of Jews had been deported from Germany and Slovakia to the over-crowded Lodz ghetto, to others in the Baltic States and White Russia, or to a number of transit camps in the Lublin area. Three-quarters of each contingent, and sometimes the whole, was destined for execution, but there was no general rule. Sometimes they were permitted some months of ghetto life, and sometimes the trains were diverted straight to the death camps.

Early in 1942 Himmler issued instructions through Eichmann and Martin Luther, director of the Foreign Office Department 'Deutschland' which was heavily implicated in the extermination of foreign Jews, for the first deportations from Western Europe. By July 1942 France, Belgium and Holland accounted for one deportation train a day, running to a timetable, while the current liquidation of the Polish ghettoes was placing too great a strain on the four existing camps. Faced with this problem Himmler attempted to establish a single clearing-house and procedure. This was at Auschwitz, in the former part of Poland annexed to Silesia, in a group of camps commanded by Rudolf Hoess, an ex-*Freikorps* man, convicted murderer and inmate of Dachau, who had become a *kapo* there and finally jumped the barrier to an S.S. commission. He was already commandant of the small Auschwitz concentration camp, when Himmler first broached to him his future role as a mass murderer, in 1941.

He experimented, late in that year, with the use of Zyklon B, blue hydrogen-cyanide crystals supplied to the camp as disinfectant gas, using it to kill a group of invalid Russian prisoners of war. So successful was it that he was ordered to adopt it permanently in March 1942, when a small gas-chamber was put into a converted barn near the evacuated Birkenwald village close to the camp site. Zyklon B impressed Himmler because there was no risk of mechanical breakdown as often happened with the diesel engines.

Finally, in the summer of 1942, Himmler decided on the use of Auschwitz as the clearing-house for Western European Jews. The single gas chamber proved totally inadequate, and four huge combined gas chamber–crematoria had been built by the autumn of 1943. But even these could not cope with six thousand bodies a day, such as occurred during the Hungarian deportations of May and June 1944; many victims had to be shot and their bodies burned in petrol-flooded trenches. Until the autumn of 1943 the numbers of transports were such that Auschwitz could not retain its monopoly, and Sobibor and Treblinka continued to function.

In the face of the Russian advance and the rebellion of surviving inmates, the Polish death camps were closed and a hideous programme of exhuming mass graves and burning the corpses carried out. Auschwitz was destroyed and no photographs survive, but enough is known of its appearance and the *modus operandi* of its staff.

Incoming trainloads were sorted, by appearance, into two groups, those for immediate extermination and those who might be employed for a time on the nearby I.G. Farben plant. Those to be murdered were taken to the gas chambers, which were surrounded by well-kept lawns and flower beds, and bore a sign indicating they were bath houses. After the victims had been marched in, the doors were sealed, and orderlies dropped the blue crystals through vents in the roof. Thirty minutes later pumps sucked out the poisonous air and the *sonderkommandos*, wearing gas-masks and rubber boots, went into action with their hoses and hooks. The corpses were conveyed to the crematoria and burned in its furnaces, the clinker was ground to ash in a mill, and the ash scattered on the waters of the Sola.

The routine of deportation and extermination went on practically until the end of the Third Reich. Much of the administrative arrangement was made by Adolf Eichmann's Gestapo sub-section for Jewish Affairs, Amt IVA4b, but clearly, numerous other interests were involved. The *Reichsbahn* provided transport as it did for slave labour, I. A. Topf and Sons, of Erfurt, won the lively competition to provide the furnaces and other crematoria equipment at Auschwitz, the firms of Tesch and Stabenow of Hamburg, and Degesch of Dassau, supplied the Zyklon B crystals at the rate of two and three-quarter tons a month. Thousands of manual and clerical workers must have known something of the business in which they were involved, but like everyone else from Himmler down, except for the S.S. camp guards, they hid from themselves the knowledge of the mass murders to which they were contributing.

The psychology of man, not only the German people, which makes mass killing by remote control possible, has the deepest significance in an age threatened by push-button warfare. The Germans are not a nation of sadists but, like any other people, they could produce enough insensitive brutes to staff the death camps, and enough administrative and clerical staff too squeamish actually to commit murder in the physical sense, but prepared to work the machinery which made it possible.

In the last months of the war the Final Solution became inextricably tangled with every other matter relating to Himmler's camp empire. Thousands of surviving camp inmates were carried west in face of the Russian advance. Hitler was ready to see them die, along with everyone else in Germany, himself included. Himmler hoped to sell their lives to the International Red Cross at the price of his own life.

The final welter of intrigue and confusion was the ultimate expression of the New Order made manifest in what the British Army discovered at Belsen. This had originally been a Star Camp for privileged Jews. There were various categories of these, demanded by a number of government agencies. The *Wehrmacht* wanted diamond-cutters and fur-dressers spared, and the Foreign

Office, the Jewish subjects of certain countries who could be used in exchange bargains with the Allies. Neither was the Gestapo averse to selling privileges for profit, as it did throughout the Final Solution, and so Belsen came into existence, Camp 2 for privileged Jews, and Camp 1 for Russian prisoners of war, both of them small.

Between January and April 1945, twenty-three transports were directed westwards to Belsen, probably due to Adolf Eichmann, who knew perfectly well what the situation was but made a last insane attempt to exterminate as many Jews as possible. On 5th February a typhus epidemic had broken out, brought by a contingent of Hungarian Jews, but despite this, and Oswald Pohl's report to Himmler who wanted, for his own reasons, to check the death rate, transports continued to pour in.

On 15th April a British detachment entered Belsen. In Camp 2 there were 15,133 people in an area intended for 7000, but no typhus and only the beginning of famine. In Camp 1, the *Haeftlingslager*, extending less than a quarter of a square mile, were 28,000 women, 12,000 men and 13,000 corpses. At least 40,000 more, largely Polish and Hungarian Jews, had died there since February, and 13,000 died within days of liberation. In a sense they had not died in vain. Had Himmler been able to control his own empire, he might have effected some last-minute concealment of its horrors; as it was the outside world learned on unimpeachable evidence the truth about the New Order.

CHAPTER TEN

Nazism in Decline

WHILE Hitler directed his war from Wolf's Lair, and his satraps busied themselves with implementing the New Order, opposition to Nazism grew. In Germany it was courageous but ineffective. More energetic and disruptive to Hitler's régime were the resistance movements in occupied Europe, but ultimately it was the military power of the Soviet Union, the U.S.A. and the British Commonwealth which destroyed the Third Reich.

Papen's Marburgh Speech is evidence of the existence of early opposition to Nazism. The motives of the man who delivered it are questionable, but the views of its authors, for which they paid with their lives, were clearly hostile to National-Socialism. But there was never a united resistance movement, still less did it win a mass following. Of the 4980 executed after July 1944, many were trimmers who had drawn back at the last moment only to find that their duplicity would not save them. A number of opposition circles existed, but the contacts between them produced little co-operation.

At one extreme the 'Kreisau Circle', which gathered round Count Helmuth James von Moltke and Peter Yorck von Wartenburg and took its name from Moltke's Silesian estates, was avowedly no more than a discussion group. Jesuits, Lutheran ministers, socialist and former trade union leaders, liberals, conservatives, landowners, academics and diplomats were members. Regarding Nazism as a passing evil, they planned the theoretical foundations of the Christian-Socialist society which should replace it. They did not lack courage, and faced execution bravely in 1944 and 1945, but they were opposed to direct action against Hitler's régime.

The difficulties of taking action and, to the 'Kreisau Circle', its futility, were demonstrated in the episode of the 'White Rose Letters'. Supported by Professor Kurt Huber of Munich University, Hans Scholl, a medical student, and Sophie, his sister, organized anti-Nazi propaganda among undergraduates. The letters which they distributed called on German youth to rebel, and they carried on despite a brutal warning from Paul Giesler, *Gauleiter* of Bavaria. Inevitably the leaders of the movement were soon found guilty of treason before the People's Court and executed. Their defiance was but one example of the numerous individual acts of heroism carried out in Nazi Germany.

More effective and, for a time, successful, was the organization labelled *Rote Kapelle*, Red Orchestra. It was an extensive espionage network transmitting intelligence to Russia over at least one hundred concealed wireless sets. *Abwehr* detected its existence, named it, and began its destruction in Brussels in December 1941. A Russian officer and his contact, a refugee Jewess, were arrested and revealed the outlines of a system controlled by the 'Grand Chef' and the 'Petit Chef', neither of whom was ever caught.

Investigation implicated Harro Schulze-Boysen as one of its ringleaders. A young man of ancient lineage, and a left-wing past, his family connections had secured for him a *Luftwaffe* commission and a job in its Intelligence Department. He developed plans for a nation-wide conspiracy and, by the time of his arrest, his influence was remarkably extensive. He had recruited Avid Harnack in the Ministry of Economics, Franz Scheliha and Horst Heilmann in the Foreign Office, and Countess Brockdorff and Frau Schumacher in the Ministry of Labour. Even in *Abwehr*, he had contacts who enabled him to avoid arrest for some time, and Bormann's Party Chancellery seems to have been the only government department which *Rote Kapelle* had not infiltrated.

The mainstream of German resistance clearly flowed from the group which began to form in the late nineteen-thirties round General Ludwig Beck, Karl Goerdeler and Ulrich von Hassell.

Goerdeler was a former *Oberbuergermeister* of Leipzig and Reich Price Controller for the first three years of Nazi government. He broke with Nazism, partly because of its anti-semitism, and from 1937 was the chief force behind resistance. Beck, Army Chief of Staff until August 1938, first opposed Hitler on purely professional grounds, but his opposition to Nazism broadened and he was nominated by the Resistance Circle as future Head of State. Hassell was ambassador to Rome until his dismissal in 1938. Until then his contempt for the vulgarity of national-socialism had not prevented him from serving it loyally, but he became its unswerving opponent. Colonel (later General) Hans Oster, Chief of Staff in *Abwehr*, was a consistently loyal member of the Circle, while there were others like Ewald von Kleist, a landowner, and Fabian von Echlabrendorff, a lawyer and wartime officer. Others involved were curiously limited in their opposition. Johannes Popitz, Acting Finance Minister for Prussia until 1944, even attempted to draw Himmler into the Resistance Circle. Admiral Canaris, head of *Abwehr*, won a posthumous reputation as a resister, but he was deeply involved in the Naujocks plot of 1939 and seemed loth to secure any clear definition of the Commissar Decree from Reinecke and 'Gestapo' Mueller. Finally there were flagrant opportunists like Artur Nebe, who may have been executed for his part in the July 1944 plot, but had, in his time, commanded an *einsatzgruppe* in Russia.

The Resistance Circle followed two methods. It hoped to attract sufficient army officers to it to accomplish a *coup d'état*, and, through contact with the Allies, obtain a compromise peace. Beck provided a link with the Army and Oster the means of concealed approaches to the Allies.

The first active conspiracy developed in the summer of 1938 when Beck was opposing Hitler's plans to attack Czechoslavakia, on the grounds that Germany would find herself involved in a European war for which she was unready. The scheme was to seize Hitler by force as soon as he gave the order to attack Czechoslovakia, and put him on trial before the People's Court. It would remain a mere paper scheme unless Brauchitsch, Army

Commander-in-Chief, and other senior generals could be persuaded that Beck's forecast was accurate. Soundings were made in London by Kleist, but he secured no evidence that Britain and France would march in defence of the Czechs. The plot hung fire and eventually petered out. The 'Zossen Conspiracy' of November 1939 was equally abortive. The conspirators played on the Army High Command's doubts about the wisdom of Hitler's plans for a campaign in the West, and there was probably even active preparation for a *putsch* at Army Headquarters in Zossen. But after an intimidating interview with the Fuehrer on 5th November, Brauchitsch and Halder, his Chief of Staff, were disinclined to go further.

As the war progressed contacts were made with the West through Sweden and Switzerland. At Whitsuntide, 1942, two Lutheran ministers, Hans Schoenfeld and Dietrich Bonhoeffer, contrived to meet Dr. Bell, the Bishop of Chichester, in Stockholm. They gave him some details of the German opposition and inquired what sort of peace the Allies would make with an anti-Nazi government, and Bell subsequently had talks with Anthony Eden, the Foreign Minister, and Sir Stafford Cripps, a leading Labour member of the War Cabinet. Hans Gisevius of *Abwehr* and others were in contact with Allen Dulles, head of the U.S. Office of Strategic Services in Switzerland after November 1942.

The Western Allies gave no response to these overtures and it is arguable that they underestimated the capacity of the German opposition. On the other hand the view, expressed in Germany since the war, that the Allies failed the Resistance Circle, by refraining from giving help, is scarcely tenable. The Germans were simultaneously putting out feelers to Stalin; the Western Allies may have known of this and had no intention of countenancing a second German-Soviet pact. Moreover, the peace terms contemplated by Geordeler were unacceptable. Well after the contacts with Bell he was seeking restoration of Germany's Eastern frontiers of 1914, retention of Austria and the Sudetenland, restoration of the South Tyrol (annexed to Italy in 1919) and autonomy for Alsace-Lorraine. He also demanded the cessation of plans for an invasion of Europe, and allied bombing raids on Germany. All but the last were clearly beyond even consideration.

By early 1943 further attempts to persuade senior army officers to get rid of Hitler had failed, and the conspirators decided that they would have to assassinate him before taking any further step. The first attempt to do so was made on 13th March 1943 when the Fuehrer visited the headquarters of Army Group Centre at Smolensk. General Henning von Tresckow and Schlabrendorff, now a lieutenant, placed a time-bomb in Hitler's plane. It was in the care of a Colonel Brandt who believed he was taking two bottles of brandy to General Stieff as a present from Tresckow. The bomb was of British design. Before handing it to Brandt, Schlabrendorff pressed a button which broke a small bottle containing a corrosive acid. The acid ate through a wire so that a spring pressed forward a striker which hit the detonator and exploded the bomb. The mechanism worked but the detonator did not fire. The next day Schlabrendorff, with incredible courage, flew to Hitler's headquarters, retrieved the bomb and substituted two bottles of brandy.

By January 1944 a further six attempts had been made to kill Hitler. Most of them were suicidal as well as homicidal. Colonel von Gersdorff attempted to assassinate the Fuehrer at the Heroes Memorial Day ceremonies in 1943, by standing next to him with bombs concealed in his overcoat pockets. The fuses needed ten minutes, but Hitler left the ceremonies ahead of his schedule and the scheme failed. In November Captain von dem Bussche was to model a new army greatcoat in Hitler's presence and intended to conceal bombs about his person, but Allied bombing raids destroyed the new uniform and the demonstration was postponed. Most of the attempts failed, as Gersdorff's had, due to Hitler's personal security technique of suddenly changing his plans without warning.

Meanwhile the Opposition suffered a setback in the destruction of *Abwehr*. Himmler's R.S.H.A. had long been eager to absorb its rival. In autumn 1942 the Gestapo arrested an *Abwehr* agent smuggling currency into Switzerland. He revealed a good deal of resistance activity, and Hans von Dohnanyi, one of the *Abwehr* plotters, was arrested and Oster obliged to resign in December 1943. During the September of that year a Gestapo agent also gained access to the anti-Nazi salon, presided over in Berlin by Frau Anna Solf, the widow of a member of the old Imperial Diplomatic Corps. It was discovered that Otto Kiep, a member of the Solf Circle, was on friendly terms with the *Abwehr* agents in Istanbul, Erich Vermehren and his wife, both of whom were hostile to Nazism. Kiep contrived to warn his friends that the Gestapo net was closing in and they fled to England. It was incorrectly believed that they had taken all the *Abwehr's* secret codes with them, and in February 1944 Hitler ordered the dissolution of *Abwehr* and its absorption by the R.S.H.A.

At this low ebb in the fortunes of the conspiracy it was joined by Klaus Philip Schenk, Count von Stauffenberg, a colonel of considerable talents, possessed of a radical temperament and a strong moral purpose. He had lost his left eye, his right hand and two fingers of his left hand in Tunisia, but undertook the task of assassinating Hitler. He was attached to the staff of General Olbricht, one of the conspirators and deputy-Commander of the *Ersatzheer*, the Home or Replacement Army. This was an organization for training recruits for active service but including a number of over-age units on garrison duty in Germany. Using as his pretext the danger of revolt by foreign workers, Stauffenberg drew up plans for the Home Army to assume emergency powers in Germany. 'Operation Valkyrie' as it was called was a detailed scheme including orders and appeals ready for the signature of Beck as new head of state and Geordeler as chancellor.

Stauffenberg made two unsuccessful attempts to kill Hitler in July 1944, but he was frequently summoned to the Fuehrer's presence to receive orders concerning the provision of new military drafts, after the end of June when he became Chief of Staff to General Fromm, Commander of the Home Army. On 20th July he flew to the Wolf's Lair, in obedience to orders, intending to make a decisive attempt on Hitler's life.

He carried with him a bomb like the one Tresckow and Schlabrendorff had used, concealed in his briefcase. It was set to explode ten minutes after the mechanism had been started. Stauffenberg was taken by Keitel into the conference room where the Fuehrer was listening to reports from the Eastern front. He placed his case under the heavy oak table, and inconspicuously withdrew from the room on the pretext of a telephone call from Berlin. Within a few minutes, at 12.42 p.m., the bomb exploded. In the confusion Stauffenberg bluffed his way through the guard posts protecting the *Wolfsschance*, boarded the plane waiting for him at the nearby airfield, and flew back to Berlin.

Meanwhile the conspirators were supposed to gather at Olbricht's office in the Bendlerstrasse. The formation of an anti-Nazi government under Beck and Goerdeler, with Field-Marshal von Witzleben as Commander-in-Chief of the Army, was to be announced. Emergency powers were to be transferred to the Army and there were detailed plans for seizing key points such as the radio station, arresting all senior party officials, and incorporating the *Waffen* S.S. into the Army. Similar *coups* were to take place in Prague, Vienna and Paris.

The success of the enterprise depended upon the assassination of Hitler and the vigorous, unhesitant execution of 'Valkyrie'. Neither condition was satisfied. Hitler emerged from the conference room burned and bruised, his right arm paralysed and his ear-drums damaged, but he was alive. The table, and chance, had saved him. The table was supported by two socles, extending nearly its whole width. Stauffenberg had left his case leaning against the inside of one of these, but after he left the room Colonel Brandt, in order to stand closer to a map, moved the case to the outside of the socle so that it absorbed much of the blast from the explosion. Shortly after 1 p.m. news reached the Bendlerstrasse that the Fuehrer was not dead and Olbricht withheld the order to begin 'Valkyrie'. He had thrown away the last chance. In the confusion at Rastenburg it was thought that the explosion had been the result of an air-raid. It was at least 2.30 p.m. before it dawned on Hitler and his entourage what Stauffenberg had tried to do, and it was probably even later when it was realized that a *putsch* had been intended. The Generals, even those who were well intentioned, had once more failed the Fatherland. Even self-interest could not destroy the unease they had felt all along at breaking their oath to Hitler. Their only hope of survival, once they had gone so far along the path of revolt, was to succeed.

Not until Stauffenberg landed at Rangsdorf airfield, still three-quarters of an hour drive from the Bendlerstrasse, at 3.45 p.m., was anything done. He supplied the drive that had been lacking, but by then it was too late. Troops were sent to occupy the government quarter of Berlin but the battalion was commanded by one Major Remer who was not a conspirator. Goebbels, the only senior Nazi in Berlin, was warned of his coming by Hans Hagen, a propaganda officer attached to the battalion. On his arrival at Goebbels's office, Remer was persuaded to answer a telephone call from Rastenburg. The unmistakable voice on the line so impressed him that he apparently stood to attention while acknowledging orders to suppress the *putsch*, and news of his immediate promotion to the rank of colonel.

Stauffenberg made desperate attempts to push the chief army commands into action, but at 6.30 p.m. German radio broadcast a message from Goebbels that Hitler was alive, and at 8.00 p.m. Keitel issued a teleprinter instruction to all commands to ignore any order not countersigned by himself or Himmler, whom Hitler had appointed to command the *Ersatzheer*. Shortly afterwards it was announced that the Fuehrer would broadcast to the German people at about midnight.

During the evening a group of officers, loyal to Hitler, whom the conspirators had arrested, escaped and released General Fromm, the Commander of the Home Army. He had also been placed in custody since his attitude to the conspirators was equivocal, and on his release he resorted to a futile attempt to save his own neck. When troops arrived at the Bendlerstrasse to arrest the conspirators he had Stauffenberg, Olbricht, Colonel Mertz and Lieutenant Haeften shot by the light of the headlamps

F

of an armoured car. Further summary executions were prevented by the arrival of Kaltenbrunner, Heydrich's successor, who was more concerned to interrogate the prisoners.

Only in Paris did the conspiracy enjoy temporary success. General Heinrich von Stuelpnagel, the Military Governor of France, loyally carried out his role and arrested 1200 S.S. and S.D. men, so that the Army was in complete control of Paris. To consolidate this position it was essential for Stuelpnagel to have the active support of the commander in the field, and here again misfortune had befallen the conspiracy. Until 17th July Field-Marshal Rommel had been Commander-in-Chief in the west, but on that day he was severely injured when his car was attacked by British fighter planes and on 20th July he lay unconscious in hospital. He had been temporarily replaced by Field-Marshal von Kluge, who had persistently evaded commitment to the Resistance Circle since 1942. Had Hitler been killed he would probably have come over, but in the circumstances refused to exploit the opportunity Stuelpnagel had created, and the *putsch* collapsed.

The manhunt which followed was inspired by a savage desire for revenge on Hitler's part. It has been estimated that 4980 people were executed after the July plot and thousands more put into concentration camps. Many officers were executed with bestial cruelty, by slow hanging in a noose of piano wire, suspended from a meat hook. The executions were filmed and shown to Hitler who watched them with satisfaction, although Goebbels was obliged to bury his face in his hands.

Hitler, whose class-consciousness had always contained a paranoiac element, further vented his spite on the aristocratic caste in whose presence he was never at ease. The *Waffen S.S.* was put on equal terms with the Army and the Nazi salute made compulsory.

In one sense the failure of the German opposition to Nazism is unimportant. The virtue of men's actions lies in their motive, and the hard core of resisters acted without regard to their chances of success. Their courage is the only decent element in the history of the Third Reich.

The scope of this book does not permit more than a passing reference to the activities of resistance groups in occupied territory. The Nazis found plenty of collaborators, and the work of the Final Solution was facilitated by the anti-semitism of conquered populations in the East. But there was always sustained underground opposition which added to the difficulties of German government and assisted Allied espionage. Like the German opposition it failed when it challenged Nazism openly, and the heroic Warsaw rising of 1944 is the outstanding example.

It was Hitler's war which destroyed the Third Reich. By attacking Russia he committed himself, in the long run, to fighting a war on two fronts, although this did not become reality until 1944. Once, he had been able to see the fatal consequence of this, but so eager was he to pursue *Lebensraum* in the East that he persuaded himself that Britain was defeated, launched 'Barbarossa', and further increased his difficulties by failure to understand the significance of the U.S.A.

The Russian counter-offensive which was launched in December 1941 was held during the following winter and the German line stabilized, but only at tremendous cost. That the line was held was almost entirely due to Hitler, who assumed personal command of the Army and specifically forbade any withdrawals. But he made a serious mistake in the next twelve months in failing to exploit and dominate the Mediterranean situation, by giving Rommel everything his Afrika Corps needed, and capturing Malta. That this could have been achieved is scarcely to be doubted, but Hitler's real interest was Russia and he showed only fitful concern for other theatres of war. During 1942, R.A.F. bombing raids on Germany began to build up, and the resources of the *Luftwaffe* were so extended in Russia that the Reich was without adequate air protection.

In the autumn of 1942 the tide of war was quite perceptibly turning against Germany. In October General Montgomery's 8th Army broke through the German lines at El Alamein and in the following month British and American troops landed in North-West Africa. By the end of November a Russian offensive on the

Stalingrad front had encircled twenty German divisions between the rivers Volga and Don. In January 1943 the German 6th Army, besieged in Stalingrad, was fought to a standstill and capitulated. From then on, except for local recoveries, the German armies in the East were either on the defensive or in retreat.

Now that it was too late, Hitler tried to retrieve the African situation and poured men across the Mediterranean despite Rommel's advice to the contrary. As a result, 250,000 men and their equipment, the entire Axis forces in North Africa, were in Allied hands by May 1943.

In July the King of Italy felt strong enough to dismiss Mussolini, and on 8th September an armistice with the Allies was announced, and simultaneously Allied armies landed on the Italian mainland and began to push north against the German troops in Italy. For a time Allied success in this theatre was checked. Mussolini, after his dismissal, had been placed under guard in a small hotel in the Abruzzi Mountains. He was dramatically rescued, on 12th September, by an S.S. detachment led by Otto Skorzeny. German arms restored him as puppet dictator of the Italian Social Republic, and at the end of the year Kesselring's armies still held the Allies on a line not far north of Naples. But this was a respite, not a success, and elsewhere the end of 1943 saw Nazism in retreat.

The Red Armies were advancing steadily towards the frontiers of Poland and Rumania, incidentally increasing the apprehension felt by Germany's Balkan satellites. Day and night the R.A.F. and U.S.A.A.F. maintained their bombing offensive, while at sea the U-boat successes of 1942 were not repeated, and the Battle of the Atlantic was clearly lost. At Casablanca in January, and Moscow in October, Churchill, Roosevelt and Stalin affirmed their intention to enforce unconditional surrender.

The first half of 1944 saw the Red Armies continuing their advances into Poland and Rumania, while Kesselring steadily gave ground in Italy. On 6th June the long awaited attack in the West began with the Normandy landings. A war on two fronts had become reality. By the end of August France was liberated, and the war came to Germany when an American patrol crossed the frontier on 11th September. But the end did not come as quickly as might have been expected. A remarkable recovery enabled the German Army to stabilize a continuous defence line west of the Rhine, Kesselring held the Allies south of the Po, and the Vistula still lay between the Soviet armies and East Prussia.

As its Empire collapsed Nazism remained unchanged. Hitler was unquestionably its Fuehrer. Increasingly immersed in military affairs, at Rastenburg, he became cut off from reality. He trusted no one, took his meals alone and had his food tasted for him before he ate it. Every misfortune was rationalized, so that the failure of the Stauffenberg plot only strengthened his belief that Providence would spare him to fulfil his historic destiny. He refused to accept or listen to unpalatable military facts, turning on his informants with threats and abuse, or delivering himself of rambling speeches about his V-bombs and U-boats. In 1943 he began to suffer from uncontrollable tremors in his left arm and leg, and severe stomach cramps, and, during the last two years of his life, seems to have been kept going by a startling variety of fake medicines, stimulants, narcotics and aphrodisiacs dispensed by his quack doctor, Theodor Morell.

Of the original leaders only Goering and Goebbels remained important, and as the war progressed Goering's power was a hollow shell. Until nearly the end he was Hitler's successor, and holder of well over twenty offices, but increasingly he relapsed into a life of sloth and luxury on his Karinhall estates, his public appearances notable only for the variety of colourful uniforms he affected. The failure of the *Luftwaffe* discredited him with the Fuehrer, and Goering avoided contact with him, waited for the end, and hoped vainly to disavow all responsibility when the war was over.

As Goering fell, Goebbels rose. In the early war years his star declined, but well before the end he had regained Hitler's confidence which he never again lost. He could even discuss ideas with the Fuehrer, but failed to persuade him to seek a compromise peace in 1943 and 1944. More realistic than Goering, he appreciated that he had no future outside the Nazi movement and became at the last as fanatical as Hitler.

The only two leaders to achieve prominence, for the first time, during the war, were Martin Bormann and Albert Speer. When Rudolf Hess flew on his eccentric peace-mission to Scotland in 1941, Bormann succeeded him as Head of the Party Chancellery. He dealt with all legislation on behalf of the Party, and controlled the appointment of party members to official jobs, and all contacts between government departments and the Party. Communication between other party offices and the Fuehrer was possible only through Bormann. The *gauleiters* were responsible to him and, in 1942, when all *gaue* became Reich Defence Districts, and the *gauleiters* Reich Defence Commissioners, he secured control of the civilian war effort. He fought a bitter conflict with that other great empire builder, Heinrich Himmler, and by the end of 1944 was winning. This was entirely due to the fact that although both men had organizations, Bormann was close to Hitler and Himmler was not. Bormann was in constant attendance at court, relieved the Fuehrer of tedious administrative tasks, and drafted nearly all his instructions.

Speer enjoyed a rapid rise to power after his appointment as Minister for Armaments Production in 1942, and became responsible for the entire war economy. His achievements were remarkable, but he became concerned at the price Germany was paying for war and early in 1945 planned, unsuccessfully, to assassinate Hitler. Thereafter he made attempts to thwart Hitler's orders, but never entirely escaped from the spell which the Fuehrer cast over his subordinates. Until the last few days of his life Hitler's hold on the Party remained intact.

At the lower levels, Nazism continued to spawn corruption of every kind. Goebbels himself said of the *gauleiters* that they 'had only to be given the old *ius primae noctis* to enjoy powers greater than those of the most absolute princes of the seventeenth and eighteenth centuries'.

Taking advantage of the temporarily stabilized situation in

autumn 1944, Hitler issued a final conscription order, calling up every able-bodied man between sixteen and sixty into the *Volkssturm*, a kind of Home Guard. He also took his last significant tactical decision. Leaving the eastern front dangerously weak, extra divisions were moved to the West, and on 16th December Field-Marshal von Rundstedt launched an offensive in the Ardennes. It never looked like reaching Antwerp, its objective, and, by Christmas, was contained.

From January 1945 onwards Germany's fate was out of her own hands. Hitler had grave difficulty in learning what was happening as the Allies moved in relentlessly from both sides. On 12th January the Russians launched their victory offensive in Poland, and in March the British and American forces crossed the Rhine. By the middle of April the Nazi Reich was a mere corridor, approximately a hundred miles wide, in the heart of Germany, and the Russians were besieging Berlin.

For some months Hitler lived in the city, spending nearly all his time in a bunker beneath the Reich Chancellery. On 22nd April he made his last decision. He would remain in Berlin, and commit suicide. Beneath the grandiose gesture the worthlessness of the man is apparent. He had led Germany into disaster, assumed day-to-day control of military affairs, rejected every suggestion that peace might serve his people best, until, at the last moment, he faced the inevitability of defeat and opted out of any responsibility for its consequences. It was the final selfish exercise of arbitrary power. Yet having implicitly abandoned power he could not bear others to wield it while he still lived. The news that Goering was contemplating overtures to the Allies, and that Himmler was actually in touch with Count Bernadotte of Sweden, aroused him to fury and they were stripped of all their offices.

On 29th April he dictated his will and political testament. Much of it was virulent anti-semitism, while the rest dealt with the unreal question of his successor. Rather surprisingly Admiral Doenitz, now Commander-in-Chief of the Navy, was nominated as President of the Reich and Supreme Commander of the Armed

Forces. Goebbels was to be Chancellor, and Bormann Party Minister. Himmler and Goering were expelled from the Party.

On the following day, at 3.30 p.m., with Russian troops only a few streets away from the Chancellery, Hitler shot himself in his suite in the Fuehrerbunker. Eva Braun, whom he had married some twelve hours before, took poison. Under the supervision of Goebbels and Bormann, the bodies were laid in a shallow trench, soaked with petrol and burned.

Bormann immediately informed Doenitz, by radio, of his nomination as Hitler's successor, but the fact that Hitler was dead was concealed for a further twenty-four hours, while Goebbels and Bormann made fruitless attempts to negotiate with the Russians. Only then was Doenitz informed, and the news was broadcast on 1st May. During that evening Goebbels poisoned his children and shot his wife and himself. Bormann attempted to leave Berlin, but whether or not he succeeded has never been established.

Doenitz's attempts to divide the Allies in the next few days were clumsy and futile. At Rheims, on 7th May, 1945, General Jodl and Admiral von Friedeburg signed the unconditional surrender of all German Forces presented to them jointly by the U.S.A., the Soviet Union, Britain and France.

The Third Reich was dead, but its aftermath dragged on for some years afterwards, in the war-criminal trials held at Nuremberg and elsewhere. Himmler and Goering committed suicide while in captivity. Ribbentrop, Keitel, Kaltenbrunner and many others went to the gallows. Albert Speer and Hess were sentenced to life imprisonment, Papen and Schacht went free. The enormous problems of resettling refugees will be completed only by death. Many victims of Nazism have remained in displaced persons camps, having nowhere else to go. The international legacy of the Third Reich remains. Its destruction brought about the confrontation in central Europe of the two great powers of the twentieth century, the United States of America and Soviet Russia. The division of Germany into two, and further division of Berlin, were the result of their meeting.

Nazism in the outward forms described here is also dead. The activities of the absurd groups who ape its manners and dress are of no account. It was a German phenomenon, a fact which need not be laboured but must be faced. It was not simply the work of one man and it is absurd to talk as if Hitler personally drove the deportation trains, recruited slave-labour, tortured suspects in the Prinz Albrechtstrasse and poured Zyklon B crystals into the gas chambers at Auschwitz.

But Nazism was a corruption and degradation of the human spirit, and the Germans are not unique in being liable to such a condition. It has been pointed out that they found active collaborators wherever they went. In essence Nazism lives on in any country, or institution, where men wield arbitrary power, where prisoners are held without trial, or the police maltreat those whom they arrest. Since German Nazism's one undeniable ideological characteristic was racialism it lives on, above all, wherever men feel themselves superior to others because of their race or colour, be it in Alabama, the English Midlands or Cape-town. It will survive and tend to flourish if mankind turns aside from it and looks the other way, as many Germans did in the nineteen-thirties and forties. In the eighteenth century Edmund Burke stated man's responsibility plainly enough : 'All that is necessary for evil to thrive, is that good men do nothing about it.'

Germany Divided

IT WAS Sir Winston Churchill who first spoke, in 1946, of the iron curtain which had fallen across Europe. In its tangible form of barbed-wire barriers it runs across Germany from the Baltic to the Austrian border. It cuts across hundreds of roads, some of them once important motorways, now overgrown for some distance either side of the barrier because access between the two Germanies is possible along only a few agreed routes.

In 1943 the wartime allies established a European Advisory Commission which, in anticipation of victory, divided Germany into occupation zones. These were accepted at Yalta in 1945. Proclamations were formulated, to be made public when the war ended, describing the structure of military government to be imposed on Germany, and the division of Berlin into four was agreed.

The circumstances of the allied invasion led to *ad hoc* arrangements being made with no reference to an overall plan, and German surrender found the allies in areas which did not always correspond to those accepted at the conference table.

In June 1945 the allied military commanders issued the Yalta proclamations. Occupation zones were defined, a Joint Control Council was established, and a four power *Kommandatura* for Berlin. During the next two months the victors assembled at Potsdam to make a number of arrangements, none of them very satisfactory. Russia annexed the northern half of East Prussia and Poland was allowed to administer eastern Germany as far west as the line of the rivers Oder and Niesse. Germans in Poland,

Czechoslovakia and Hungary were to be evacuated to Germany and 'equitably distributed' among the four occupation zones. Germany was to be treated as a single economic unit. Less precise statements were issued about de-nazification, demilitarization and reparations.

The Joint Control Commission failed to achieve anything positive. Russia and France persistently refused to treat Germany as an economic whole, and the country revived as four separate areas. In the south the Americans pursued a vigorous policy of de-nazification, and encouraged the re-birth of democratic institutions as quickly as possible. The British, in the north, were less active in these fields, and pursued a pragmatic policy in order to provide essential public services again as soon as possible. The French in the south-west, and the Russians in the east, sought the spoils of conquest, France, for some time, aspired to annexe the Saar, while the Soviet government actively seized reparations, began a programme of land reform ultimately leading to collectivization, and ostensibly encouraged the redevelopment of democratic political life.

The amalgamation of the British and American zones for economic purposes in 1946 was a clear stage in the collapse of the Joint Control Commission. Russian refusal to participate in the American Marshall Aid programme for European recovery, in 1947, aggravated the situation. In the following year French policy was modified, and the three western zones became an economic unit. At the same time a scheme for currency reform was introduced in the West, and Russia took this as her occasion for withdrawing from the Control Commission. A few days later the Berlin blockade began, and only a tremendous airlift, begun on the initiative of General Lucius Clay, kept the western sector of Berlin supplied between May 1948 and March 1949. Meanwhile preparations were in hand to establish self-government in West Germany, and in May 1949 the German Federal Republic was proclaimed in Bonn. The initial limitations on its powers were all removed by 1955, when it became a sovereign state. The German Democratic Republic was proclaimed in the East shortly after the establishment of the Federal Republic. It was a Russian creation and has remained a Russian satellite.

The Reich has vanished. The sandy heathland of Brandenburg, the nucleus of the Hohenzollern Empire, is in East Germany. East Prussia, overrun by the Teutonic Knights in the twelfth century, and acquired by the Hohenzollerns four hundred years later, is divided between Poland and Russia. West Prussia, seized at the first partition of Poland in 1772, is once more under Polish administration. Eastern Pomerania, which the Great Elector won at Westphalia in 1648, and Western Pomerania, which his grandfather wrested from Sweden early in the eighteenth century, are divided between East Germany and Polish administration. Silesia, which Frederick the Great fought for twice, is in Polish hands. The one-time Hohenzollern possessions in the Rhineland, and the areas welded to Brandenburg-Prussia by Bismarck's policy of 'blood and iron', make up the Federal Republic.

Since the war West Germany has undergone a remarkable political and economic recovery. A stable democracy seems to have been established by the Bonn basic law of 1949. It provides for a federal constitution and there are ten states in the Republic in addition to West Berlin. The Bundestag, the lower legislative chamber, is elected by direct universal suffrage, and the members of the Bundesrat, the upper house, are appointed by the state parliaments in proportion to population. The Bundestag has the greater share of legislative power, but the Bundesrat has a suspensive veto. The President, who holds office for five years and is re-eligible only once, is chosen by a Convention of the Bundestag plus an equal number of representatives chosen by the state parliaments. The Chancellor is elected by the Bundestag on the nomination of the President. An interesting item is Article 24 of the constitution which provides for the transfer of sovereign powers to international institutions, should this be thought desirable.

Similar in some ways to the defective Weimar Constitution, the Bonn law is sufficiently different for stable government to have been achieved through it. The central government has tended to increase in power since 1949, and there is no unduly powerful state such as Prussia. The President's position is little more than decorative, and there is no equivalent to the notorious Article 48 of the Weimar. The Chancellor is more secure than before 1933. The Bundestag can express no confidence in him only if it simultaneously nominates a successor.

Nor has there been undue proliferation of parties. The Christian Democratic Union and the Social Democratic Party have been the two most important. Coalition government, between the C.D.U. and the less powerful Federal Democratic Party, has at times been necessary, but it has not proved to be the only means of providing viable government. In 1953 the C.D.U. won a small overall majority.

Political life has been relatively placid, with rearmament and foreign policy being the issues which have most clearly marked differences between the parties. The S.P.D. opposed the policy of rearmament successfully pursued by Konrad Adenauer, the first Chancellor and leader of the C.D.U. Under the leadership of Kurt Schumacher, the S.P.D. also opposed Adenauer's policy of alignment with the West, on the grounds that a neutral Germany would be less likely to antagonize the Soviet Union, and thus facilitate re-unification. Since Schumacher's death in 1952 this unrealistic appraisal of the situation has been considerably modified, and any future S.P.D. administration in Germany is no more likely to withdraw from N.A.T.O. than a Labour government in Britain. West Germany's economic prosperity has done much to steal traditional socialist thunder since 1945, and the S.P.D. no longer appears wedded to a doctrinaire policy of nationalization.

Adenauer contributed significantly to the successful development of West Germany since the war. He had been Mayor of Cologne from 1917 to 1933, and a member of the old Centre party. Deprived of office by the Nazis, he lived in retirement until 1945, when he became once more the Mayor of Cologne, only to be deposed again, this time by the British occupation authorities. He was the founder of the C.D.U., and his considerable political talent quickly won him respect, if not always popularity.

His pro-western policy has made Germany an effective member of N.A.T.O. and the E.E.C., and, more strikingly, created friendship between Germany and France for the first time since 1870.

Finally, economic prosperity, with a rising standard of living and consistently low unemployment figures, has materially eased the early years of the Federal Republic.

How far these factors have created democracy as well as stable government it is impossible to know. Adenauer was instinctively authoritarian. It has also been suggested that the tone of political life under him suffered from the lack of clear principle which was characteristic of the old Centre party. The first Federal Chancellor certainly became a father figure, and fears were expressed about the fate of Germany when he eventually gave up office. It has been reported that one S.P.D. member of the Bundestag expressed his unwillingness to press so venerable a figure too hard in debate. None of this reflects a healthy democratic situation. The outlawing of the Communist party suggests a lack of confidence in the power of liberal democracy to survive on its own merits, and there have been occasions when press criticism appears to have been dealt with in an authoritarian manner. At present the Federal Republic can have absorbed little more of the traditions of parliamentary democracy than did the Weimar Republic. Continued material affluence will ensure stability, but it will do nothing to teach people what Hitler always appreciated: the primacy of political over economic power. The right to vote, and to seek public office on equal terms with other men, are too readily taken for granted in a society given over to the pursuit of material goods.

The chief architect of West Germany's remarkable economic recovery has been Ludwig Erhard, now Federal Chancellor, and formerly Minister of Economics in Adenauer's government. He built up a free market economy, which included the expenditure of public money on the usual social services. Several factors contributed to his success. Much of Germany's pre-war industrial plant had been destroyed by allied bombing, and today most of her factories are modern in design and equipment. Three billion dollars were received through Marshall Aid, and a constant flow of refugees from the East helped to supply an urgently needed reservoir of manpower. For some years Germany had no re-armament programme to fulfil, so making more public money available for other purposes. Most workers are members of one large union organization, the *Deutscher Gewerkschaftsbund*, and during the occupation the policy of co-determination was adopted, so that employees have a voice in policy decisions. In many large corporations one director is chosen to represent the interests of the employees, and this seems to have reduced the number of serious industrial conflicts to very few in the post-war years.

Nazism shows no sign of reviving, although there have been occasions when the Germans have not altogether disavowed it. The C.D.U. thought it politically useful to attack Willy Brandt, the socialist Mayor of West Berlin, on the grounds that during the war he had taken Norwegian citizenship and fought actively against Nazi Germany in the Norwegian resistance. But the Federal government has been assiduous in bringing to trial former Nazis accused of war crimes.

No fresh legal proceedings are to be instituted against Nazi war criminals after May 1965. This decision has aroused a certain amount of opposition both inside and outside Germany. It is based on a statute of limitations, which was first used in 1870 when the expectation of life was appreciably lower than it is now. It is argued that no special legislation should be passed in order to circumvent existing law in this case, since it would contravene the principle of equality before the law. Indeed, the Nazi régime was based on special laws, and the Federal govern-ment should avoid following such a precedent.

Dr. Adenauer has spoken in favour of extending the twenty-year limit, and there are strong arguments in favour of doing so. There are still untraced Nazi war criminals, although how many there are is uncertain. The Polish and Israelia governments assert that there are thousands, but in West Germany official sources suggest only a few. Even if a low estimate is correct, it would

need only a few cases of savagery to be revealed too late to provoke a wave of hostility towards Germany. It is also doubtful
whether the legal argument against introducing exceptional legislation is valid. It is not necessary for proceedings to have been
completed by May 1965; they have only to be instituted by then,
so that consequent trials will probably last beyond 1970.

Concrete measures have been adopted to atone for Nazi persecution of the Jews. Federal law forbids racial or religious dis-
crimination. Millions of marks have been awarded in restitution
to German Jews, or their heirs, who suffered persecution, although
this has not been extended to Austrian Jews, and firms like
Krupps have avoided paying anything more than nominal com-
pensation to their former Jewish slaves. The government has
invited Jews to return to Germany and has financed the rebuilding of synagogues. A reparations agreement was signed with
Israel in 1952 under which large quantities of machinery, agricultural equipment and so on have been supplied to the Jewish state.

That there is still anti-semitism in Germany is not to be
doubted, but so there is in every other country in Europe. The
outbreak of swastika daubing, and the painting of abusive re-
marks on synagogue walls in late 1959 and early 1960, began in
West Germany but spread rapidly in other western European
countries. The Bonn government was quick to express strong
distaste for such activity and many German offenders were imprisoned. In Germany, as elsewhere, it is true that many who
were guilty of such activity were juvenile delinquents, with a
taste for notoriety and little understanding of the significance of
what they did. It is also true that such people are the raw
material of any political movement based on intolerance and a
disregard for human dignity.

Less can be said of the Democratic Republic, for less is known.
The constitution has a liberal appearance, but this is no more
than a façade. The original federal character has disappeared, now
that the states and their parliaments have been replaced by fourteen administrative districts, with no powers of initiative. It is a
one party state at the head of which is Walter Ulbricht, a lifelong

communist who spent the Nazi era in Moscow from where, it is to be assumed, he still takes his orders.

Economically, East Germany has also prospered, but not so dramatically as the West. It enjoys agricultural self-sufficiency, but its industrial situation was damaged by the division of Germany into two. Before the war it possessed only secondary industries which depended for coal and steel on the Ruhr. Apart from some copper and brown coal it has little by way of raw materials, and there is no reliable information about the extent to which it has proved possible to stimulate industrial output. Nor is it clear how far the East Germans are reconciled to Communist government. Western propaganda has tended to make much of the strikes and riots that occurred in East Berlin and other towns in the summer of 1953. These seem to have been provoked when workers on the new apartment buildings in East Berlin had their daily production quotas raised without any increase in wages. The riots were suppressed by force, including the use of tanks. But that happened more than a decade ago and is scarcely valid evidence for the state of mind of the East Germans today.

The steady flow of refugees from east to west is the other item of evidence commonly used to suggest how much better life is in Western Germany. The refugee problem is one which the two Germanies have in common. During 1964, 3155 East Germans, most of them under 25, fled to the West. They crawled through tunnels, crossed minefields, hedgehopped in stolen aircraft, swam the Elbe, and scaled the Berlin wall under fire. In the same year the East German government allowed thirty thousand of its people to settle in the Federal Republic under a scheme to re-unite families on compassionate grounds. But it is significant that most of these were old people. Ulbricht has every intention of keeping his supplies of manpower.

It would be wrong, however, to present the refugee situation from only one side. During November and early December 1964, 295,000 pensioners were allowed to visit their relatives in the West. Of these only 220 remained. Television and newspaper interviews showed that most of the visitors had no intention of uprooting themselves for a life in the West. There is also a steady flow of refugees from West to East, and 4682 Germans moved to the Democratic Republic in 1963, more than came from the East in the following year. But it should be remembered that the journey eastwards can be accomplished in a conventional manner, and is not restricted to the physically daring.

There is still a steady flow of immigrants from the Eastern block countries into West Germany. Since 1950 there have been 538,000, many of them from the former German territories beyond the Oder–Niesse line, now under Polish administration. The West German government has recently claimed that there are some 'hundreds of thousands' of Germans still in Poland who wished to leave. In principle the Polish government is not opposed to this, but, like East Germany, has no desire to lose skilled manpower.

The refugee problem is, in fact, insoluble. It is bound up with the increasingly unrealistic problem of the re-unification of Germany. All German politicians pay lip service to this aim. West German spokesmen still assert claims to the land across the Oder–Niesse. To renounce the ideal of unification would probably be political suicide, although there is no possibility of it becoming reality in the foreseeable future. The older generation of Germans prefers to cling to its myth, like the British to their vanished Empire. New generations will not be caught in an attitude of mind which they know to be unrealistic but cannot change. Very soon the first post-war generation of Germans will be politically enfranchised, and the division of Germany will mean little more to them, perhaps, than India to their British contemporaries.

At present the failure to accept the German situation has created a number of anomalies. None of the wartime allies has signed a peace treaty with either of the two Germanies, since this would imply acquiescence in the present situation, with which everyone expresses at least formal dissatisfaction. Russia has extended formal recognition to the Federal Republic, although the Western allies do not recognize East Germany. Neither of the two Germanies thus has a seat in the United Nations.

Perhaps it is the existence of Berlin which perpetuates the ideal of unification more than anything else. West Berlin is an enclave in the heart of East Germany, containing over two million hostages to Communism. There have been three major Berlin crises since the war. The first was the blockade of 1948–9, and the others occurred in 1958 and 1961. Ostensibly on each occasion the Russians have hoped to expel the western powers who have succeeded in holding on to an apparently untenable position. In fact Russian policy has changed considerably. It is probably true that Stalin intended to obtain Berlin as part of his wider schemes for European domination. But Khruschev's policy on the two subsequent occasions was to use the Berlin situation as a means to force the United States and her allies to conclude a general European settlement. Ulbricht may have hoped for the resources of West Berlin in 1961, but the Berlin Wall, built on Russian orders, surely suggests Russian acceptance of the situation rather than any immediate intention of altering it.

On each occasion the West has reduced the conflict to the purely local question of who should occupy Berlin, to which the answer is not in doubt. Both sides accept the present situation. It is the wider implications of the Berlin problem that contain the potential seeds of world conflict, and the Russians are in a position to exploit this whenever it suits their policy.

Germany is thus heavily involved in the Cold War, and her division symbolizes the division of the whole world. Any notion that Germany should fulfil the role of a neutral zone in central Europe is out of the question. Both Germanies are firmly aligned on opposite sides of the political fence. Whether they can become a permanent free zone, which is a much canvassed idea, remains to be seen. The fears expressed in some circles at German rearmament seem rooted in the past, rather than based on present realities and Germany can hardly be regarded as a threat to peace in the sense that she was before 1939. In the Federal Republic democratic government is established at least more firmly than at any previous time in German history. In a world so divided it is encouraging to perceive room for some optimism.

Chronological Table of Events

1918

November 3. German revolution began with a naval mutiny at Kiel.
November 9. Abdication of the Kaiser.
      Proclamation of the German Republic.
      Ebert–Groener Pact. The Army agrees to co-operate with the
      provisional government.
November 11. Cessation of hostilities on the Western Front.

1919

February 6. National Assembly met at Weimar.
June 28. Versailles Treaty signed (ratified by Germany on July 7).
July 31. Adoption of the Weimar constitution.
September 16. Hitler joined the German Workers Party.

1920

March 13–17. The Kapp *Putsch*.
April 1. Foundation of the N.S.D.A.P. (Nazi Party).

1923

This year saw the collapse of the mark.
January 11. French reoccupation of the Ruhr.
November 8–9. Beer Hall *Putsch* in Munich, followed by the imprison-
ment of Hitler and a ban on the Nazi Party.

1924

April 16. Germany accepts the Dawes Plan for an international loan and
revised reparation payments.
December 12. Hitler released from the Landsberg Fortress Prison.

1925

January 4. Bavarian state government lifted the ban on the Nazi Party.

February 26. Reappearance of the *Voelkischer Beobachter.*
February 27. Nazi Party officially refounded. From then until 1930 was the period during which its complex organization was built up in preparation for the seizure of power.
October 5–16. Locarno conference (Treaty signed December 1).
November 9. First S.S. unit established.

1926

May 18. First meeting of the Preparatory Commission of the Geneva Disarmament Conference.
September 8. Germany admitted to the League of Nations.

1929

June 1. Himmler became S.S. Leader, and Goebbels propaganda leader.
June 7. Young Plan for reduced reparation payments published. A bitter campaign was launched against it by Hugenberg and Hitler in which the latter became a nationally known figure for the first time.
October. Collapse of the Wall Street Stock Exchange in New York marked the beginning of an economic depression which affected the whole of western Europe.
December 22. German referendum in favour of accepting the Young Plan.

1930

March 27. Bruening became Chancellor.
July 16. Bruening began to govern under Article 48 of the constitution.
September 14. Nazis won first major electoral victory. The number of their seats in the Reichstag rose from 12 to 107.
September. 3,000,000 unemployed in Germany.

1931

March 20. Projected Austro-German Customs Union.
September. 4,350,000 unemployed in Germany.
September 5. World Court ruled that the projected customs union was contrary to international agreement.
October 10. Hitler's first abortive interview with Hindenburg.
November. Further Nazi successes in state elections.

1932

January. 6,000,000 unemployed in Germany.
February–July. First session of the Geneva Disarmament Conference.
February 25. Hitler became a German citizen.
March 13. Indecisive presidential election.
April 10. Hindenburg defeated Hitler in presidential election.
April 13. Ban on the S.A.
May 30. Bruening resigned as Chancellor.
May 31. Papen became Chancellor.

June 14. Ban on the S.A. was lifted.

July 17. Altona riots.

July 20. Papen suppressed democratic forms of government in Prussia.

July 31. Nazis won 230/608 seats in the Reichstag.

August 13. Hindenburg refused to appoint Hitler as Chancellor.

November 6. Number of Nazi seats in the Reichstag reduced to 196.

November 17. Resignation of Papen as Chancellor.

December 2. Schleicher became Chancellor.

1933

January 28. Schleicher resigned.

January 30. Hitler was appointed as Chancellor.

February 27. Reichstag Fire.

February 28. Suspension of guarantees of individual liberty.

March 5. Last theoretically free elections. Nazis won 288 seats.

March 23. Enabling Law passed.

April 1. National boycott of Jewish shops and businesses began.

April 7. Civil Service Law. Non-Aryan teachers, officials, etc., obliged to resign.

May 2. Trades Unions banned.

May 17. Strikes and lock-outs forbidden.

June 1. Hitler placed a 1,000 mark tax on visas for entry into Austria, in order to damage the Austrian tourist trade.

June 19. Austrian government banned the Nazi Party in Austria.

July 11. German Protestant churches amalgamated as the Evangelical Church.

July 14. Nazi Party declared the only legal political party.

July 20. German Concordat with the Papacy.

September 22. Burning of the books began.

October 14. German withdraway from the Geneva Conference.

October 23. German withdrawal from the League of Nations.

1934

January 26. German-Polish non-aggression pact.

January 30. Legislation to destroy federal autonomy in Germany was completed.

March 17. Rome Protocols strengthened Austro-Italian relations.

May 3. Establishment of the People's Court.

June 14. First meeting of Hitler and Mussolini at Venice.

June 29-30. The 'Roehm Purge'.

July 25. Abortive Nazi *putsch* in Vienna. Murder of Dollfuss.

August 2. Death of Hindenburg. Hitler assumed his powers. Army took an oath of allegiance to the Fuehrer.

October 24. Constitution of the Nazi Labour Front issued.

1935

March 16. Reintroduction of conscription in Germany.

April 11. Stresa Conference (Britain, France, Italy) deplores Germany's abrogation of the rearmament clauses in the Versailles Treaty.

May 5. Reich Secret Defence Law.

June 18. Anglo-German Naval agreement.

July 11. Austro-German agreement.

September 15. Nuremberg Laws discriminating against the Jews.

October 3. Italian invasion of Abyssinia.

1936

March 7. German remilitarization of the Rhineland broke the Locarno Treaty.

May 9. Italian annexation of Abyssinia.

July 16. Outbreak of the Spanish Civil War.

October 19. German Four Year Economic Plan issued.

October 25–27. Formation of the Rome–Berlin Axis.

November 18. Germany recognized Franco's insurgent government in Spain.

December 25. German-Japanese Anti-Comintern Pact.

1937

November 5. Military conference recorded in the controversial Hossbach Memorandum.

November 6. Italy joined the Anti-Comintern Pact.

November 24. Walther Funk replaced Schacht as Minister of Economics.

1938

February 12. Schuschnigg visited Hitler at Berchtesgaden.

March 12. German invasion of Austria began.

March 13. Proclamation of the *Anschluss*.

April 10. Austria incorporated into the Reich as a new state.

April 24. Henlein, leader of the Sudeten Nazis, presented the Czech government with a series of demands for Sudeten autonomy, etc.

August 3. Lord Runciman arrived as British mediator in Prague.

September 12. Hitler demanded self-determination for the Sudetens.

September 15. Hitler–Chamberlain meeting at Berchtesgaden over the Czech crisis.

September 22–23. Second Hitler–Chamberlain meeting at Godesberg.

September 29. Munich Agreement. German annexation of the Sudetenland.

November 9. First organized pogrom in Germany.

1939

March 10–16. Annihilation of the Czech state. Establishment of the Protectorate of Bohemia and Moravia.

August 24. Nazi–Soviet Pact.

September 1. German invasion of Poland.

September 3. Britain and France declared war on Germany.

September 28. Russo-German agreement on the division of Poland.
October. Beginning of R.K.F.D.V. resettlement activities.
November. Abortice 'Zossen' conspiracy against Hitler.

1940

April 9. German invasion of Norway and Denmark.
April 30. First Polish ghetto established at Lodz.
May 10. German invasion of France and the Low Countries.
June 10. Italy declared war on Britain and France.
June 22. Franco-German armistice.
September. Critical month in the Battle of Britain.
September 27. German-Italian-Japanese Three Power Pact.
October 28. Italy invaded Greece.
November 20. Hungary joined the Axis alliance.
November 23. Rumania joined the Axis alliance.

1941

March. Hitler's directive for the treatment of occupied Russia.
April 5. German invasion of Yugoslavia and Greece.
May. Commissar Decree issued in accordance with Hitler's March instructions.
June. Jurisdiction Order issued.
June 22. German invasion of Russia.
　　　　At some time in the summer or autumn the Fuehrer Order on the Final Solution was given.
　　　　During the autumn Chelmno, the first gassing establishment, was opened near Lodz.
November 25. Bulgaria joined the Axis alliance.
December. Night and Fog Decree became operative in Western Europe.
December 7. Japan attacked U.S. and British possessions in the Pacific.
December 8. U.S.A. declared a state of war with Japan.
December 11. Germany and Italy declared war on the U.S.A.
December 19. Hitler assumed command of the German Army in the field.

1942

The 'Rote Kapelle' conspiracy against Nazi government was destroyed during the year.
'Medical' experiments began in the concentration camps, continuing until 1944.
January 20. Gross Wannsee conference at which Heydrich, Eichmann and others discussed details of the Final Solution.
March. Auschwitz began to function as a death camp using Zyklon B.
March–July. Belsec, Sobibor and Treblinka death camps established.
May 29. Heydrich mortally wounded by members of the Czech resistance..
　　　　This was followed by severe reprisals, notably the razing of Lidice.
November 4. End of the Battle of El Alamein.

1943

January 14–24. Anglo-American Conference at Casablanca. It was decided to exact unconditional surrender from the Axis Powers.

January 30. Surrender of the German 6th Army at Stalingrad.

February. The 'White Rose Letters' opposition group to Nazism arrested and executed.

March 13. Unsuccessful attempt to assassinate Hitler by a group of Army officers.

July 10. Allied armies landed in Sicily.

July 26. Mussolini arrested and imprisoned by new government in Italy.

September 2. Allied armies landed in Italy.

September 15. Mussolini proclaimed the Italian Fascist Republic, following his rescue by an S.S. detachment.

September 9. Legitimate Italian government surrendered.

September 11. German armies in Italy seized the main towns and continued to fight.

1944

February. *Abwehr* was absorbed by the R.S.H.A.

June 6. Allied landings in Normandy.

July 20. Failure of the Stauffenberg plot to assassinate Hitler. This was followed by massive reprisals lasting until nearly the end of the war.

August 24. Liberation of Paris.

September 12. American troops crossed the German frontier.

1945

January. Russian offensive overruns Poland.

February 5. Outbreak of typhus at Belsen camp.

February 7. Meeting of the heads of allied states at Yalta.

March 7. Allied armies crossed the Rhine.

April 15. British troops entered Belsen camp.

April 20. Russian troops entered the outskirts of Berlin.

April 25. American and Russian troops met at Torgau on the Elbe.

April 28. Mussolini was captured and executed by Italian partisans. The German divisions in Italy surrendered unconditionally.

April 30. Hitler committed suicide.

May 7. Provisional German government of Admiral Doenitz surrendered unconditionally.

Suggestions for Further Reading

A. Bullock: *Hitler — A Study in Tyranny* (revised edition), London, 1962.
A. Hitler: *Mein Kampf* (translated by J. Murphy), London, 1939.
T. Prittie: *Germans against Hitler*, London, 1964.
H. Rauschning: *Germany's Revolution of Destruction*, London, 1939.
G. R. Reitlinger: *The Final Solution*, London, 1953.
G. R. Reitlinger: *The S.S. — Alibi of a Nation*, London, 1956.
W. L. Shirer: *The Rise and Fall of the Third Reich*, London, 1960.
A. J. P. Taylor: *The Origins of the Second World War* (A controversial analysis), London, 1961.
H. R. Trevor-Roper: *The Last Days of Hitler* (revised edition), London, 1962.

Novels

R. Hughes: *The Fox in the Attic.*
C. Isherwood: *Goodbye to Berlin.*
T. Mann: *Dr. Faustus.*

Index